INSIGHTS
INTO
AFRICAN EDUCATION

The Karl W. Bigelow Memorial Lectures

KARL W. BIGELOW

INSIGHTS
INTO
AFRICAN EDUCATION

The Karl W. Bigelow Memorial Lectures

Edited by
Andrew Taylor
University College, Cardiff

Teachers College, Columbia University
New York and London   1984

These lectures were delivered and this book published with the support of funds provided by the Carnegie Corporation of New York.

Published by Teachers College Press, 1234 Amsterdam Avenue, New York, N.Y. 10027

LB
2193
. N393
I 57
1984

Library of Congress Cataloging in Publication Data

Main entry under title:

Insights into African education.

    1.   Bigelow, Karl W. (Karl Worth)—Addresses, essays, lectures.   2.   Columbia University. Teachers College—Faculty—Biography—Addresses, essays, lectures.
3.   College teachers—New York (State)—Biography—Addresses, essays, lectures.   4.   Education, Higher—Africa—Addresses, essays, lectures.   5.   Teachers—Training of—Africa—Addresses, essays, lectures.
I.   Bigelow, Karl W. (Karl Worth)   II.   Taylor, Andrew, M.A.
LB2193.N393157   1984   370'.96   84-158

ISBN 0-8077-2703-2

Grateful acknowledgment is made for permission to reprint the following:

Lines from "Song of Lowino," in Okot p'Bitel, *Africa's Cultural Revolution* (Nairobi: East African Publishing House, 1973). Reprinted with permission.

Lines from "Biography" are reprinted with permission of Macmillan Publishing Company from POEMS of John Masefield. Copyright 1912 by Macmillan Publishing Co., Inc., renewed 1940 by John Masefield. Reprinted also with the permission of The Society of Authors as the literary representative of the Estate of John Masefield.

Manufactured in the United States of America

89 88 87 86 85 84   1 2 3 4 5 6

Contents

Foreword

This book is a tribute to Karl W. Bigelow, who died on April 2, 1980. He joined the faculty of Teachers College, Columbia University in 1936, and remained actively associated with the College until shortly before his death. Though he became Professor Emeritus in 1963, he directed the Afro-Anglo-American Program until 1969. Thereafter, he continued to serve as an adviser to his colleagues at Teachers College, to the Overseas Liaison Committee of the American Council on Education, to the Association for Teacher Education in Africa, and to other organizations concerned with education in Africa.

Karl Bigelow was trained as an economist. However, as his career developed, he became concerned about the ways in which educators are trained for their professional roles. He was a critic and reformer of teacher education programs, a proponent of reform in the undergraduate curricula of colleges and universities through the development of integrative general education programs, a developer and implementer of training programs for college and university administrators, and an initiator of programs for the strengthening and modernizing of teacher education in English speaking Africa. These interests were overlapping and complementary, but in the last thirty years of his life his energies were devoted increasingly to matters concerned with African education. Through his teaching and writings, through his participation on influential commissions and task forces, and through the warm personal relationships which he quickly developed wherever he worked, Karl Bigelow exerted strong national and international leadership in educational forums.

This volume commemorates Karl Bigelow's African interests. In the months following his death, his friends discussed a variety of means for honoring him. The idea of a series of memorial lectures on African education was first proposed by a group of Karl's British friends and the plan was enthusiastically endorsed by his associates in the United States. Planning committees were established in both countries, and colleagues in Africa were consulted.

In the United Kingdom, the planning committee consisted of the following persons: Reginald Honeybone, Ian Maxwell, John Lewis, Andrew Taylor, Jack Thornton, John Cameron, William Dodd, John Turner, and Peter Williams. Advice was also sought from Sir Christopher Cox and Margaret Reed. Andrew Taylor graciously volunteered to compile and edit this memorial volume.

In the United States, a committee was established that included R. Freeman Butts, C. W. de Kiewiet, Carl L. Graham, Charles H. Lyons, Roger A. Myers, James R. Sheffield, Stephen H. Stackpole, and Kenneth H. Toepfer. Alan Pifer and David Hood of the Carnegie Corporation of New York were also consulted, and the Carnegie Corporation generously provided funding to help defray the costs of the lectures and of this volume.

In Uganda, W. Senteza Kajubi of Makerere University assisted with the planning and consented to deliver the New York lecture. In Nigeria, S. O. Olayide, Vice Chancellor of the University of Ibadan, and P. A. I. Obanya, Director of that university's Institute of Education, generously made arrangements for Dr. Thompson's lecture in Ibadan.

All of the individuals and institutions named contributed to the success of this project. However, particular thanks are owed to R. Freeman Butts, W. Senteza Kajubi, and A. R. Thompson, who graciously agreed to prepare and deliver the lectures. And we are all deeply indebted to Karl W. Bigelow, whose accomplishments and friendship meant so much to us over the years.

—Kenneth H. Toepfer
Professor of Higher Education and Provost,
Teachers College, Columbia University

Preface

This volume, the inspiration for which owes much to the strong enthusiasm of Peter Williams of the Department of Educational Development in Developing Countries and his colleagues in the Institute of Education, University of London, seeks to place on permanent record a tribute to a man whose warm and friendly personality, untiring energy, and well-developed sense of optimism and humour did much to weld together the disparate elements of African, British, and American teacher educators at a particularly formative period in African history. His ability to overcome the issues of nationalism, backed by the benign support of the Carnegie Corporation of New York and the strong support of Teachers College, Columbia University, and the Institute of Education, University of London, resulted in a unique partnership that ultimately involved all the University Institutes and Departments of Education in Angle-phone Africa in a close partnership, initially through the Afro-Anglo-American Program for Teacher Education in Africa. The partnership ultimately developed into the Association for Teacher Education in Africa. Through the program the new and developing institutions in Africa gained support from colleagues from overseas and were enabled to give newly appointed local staff opportunities for overseas higher degree studies and to make visits to most institutions throughout the continent, south of the Sahara and north of the Limpopo.

This led to long-standing friendships, deeper understanding of each other's problems, and a resultant friendly working relationship with university institutions in both the United Kingdom and the United States of America. These subsequently have proved to be a great asset in the development of a wide range of international programs devoted to education in general and to teacher education in particular. Such programs have characterized the African scene since the late 1950s. In these university staff, government officials, representatives of voluntary agencies, teachers, philanthropic organizations, and international agencies have all played a part.

The guiding spirit behind much of this ability to work together in confidence undoubtedly stems from Karl W. Bigelow who with his beloved wife, Margaret, so tragically stricken down in 1960, was an excellent ambassador for his university and his country and was a man to be remembered.

The volume is divided into two sections. The first contains three tributes, one from Carl L. Graham, Karl Bigelow's long-time associate; one from Africa in the person of A. Babs Fafunwa, a Nigerian who gained much of his academic training in the U.S.A.; and the third from W. A. Dodd, formerly a British colonial educational official, member of the staff of the Institute of Education, University of London, and later adviser in education to the British Overseas Development Agency. Together they typify elements of the partnership that developed.

The second part consists of the three memorial lectures, the first by W. Senteza Kajubi of Uganda, delivered at Teachers College, Columbia University; the second by A. R. Thompson of Bristol University, formerly a Colonial Education Officer in East Africa, a member of the staff of the Institute of Education, University of London, and latterly of Bristol University, and delivered at the University of Ibadan. The third lecture was delivered by R. Freeman Butts, long-time colleague of Karl Bigelow at Teachers College, Columbia, and himself distinguished in the field of international education, delivered at the Institute of Education, University of London. The order is symbolic of the partnership that developed in the Afro-Anglo-American Program.

I myself was one of the original group that drew up the program for submission to the Carnegie Corporation of New York and was in the early days, with Karl Bigelow and John Lewis, a member of the Steering Committee while serving in the Universities of Ghana and Ibadan.

—Andrew Taylor
Professor and Head, Department of Education,
and Dean, Faculty of Education,
University College, Cardiff

TRIBUTES
TO
KARL W. BIGELOW

To Remember
Karl W. Bigelow

CARL L. GRAHAM
Project Officer, UNICEF
Kampala, Uganda

Karl Worth Bigelow, who died in New York on April 2, 1980, was born in Bangor, Maine, in 1898. He received his B.A. degree from Clark University in 1920, and, after teaching for several years, he went on to Harvard University where he received his Ph.D. in economics in 1929. During his long and distinguished career, he was an outstanding teacher, an educational innovator, an administrative leader, an adviser to national and international organizations, and a remarkable human being.

THE TEACHER

He was instructor and professor of economics and sociology for a period of sixteen years at Cornell University, Harvard University and Radcliffe College, and the University of Buffalo.

After one year as visiting professor at Teachers College, Columbia University, in 1936, he was appointed professor of education, but went on leave for special assignments, one year as a consultant to the General Education Board, and six years as director of the Commission on Teacher Education, American Council on Education. From 1947 to 1963 Karl was professor of higher education at Teachers College, training future administrators of universities and colleges.

THE EDUCATIONAL INNOVATOR

As an educational innovator, Karl Bigelow was influential in the reform of American teacher education; in the introduction of "general education" as a broad-based, core curriculum for liberal arts colleges in the United States after World War II; in promoting the interests of UNESCO in the United States and abroad; in utilizing new methods of training American university and college administrators, notably, the use of the case study technique; and during his last of several "careers," in involving American institutions in promoting the interests of African higher education, in particular, teacher education.

THE ADMINISTRATIVE LEADER

His first administrative post was as headmaster of the Park School in Buffalo, a private secondary school, 1933–1935. This brought him to the attention of the president of Teachers College and, thus, to his career in teacher education.

Perhaps providentially, coincident with the death of his beloved wife, Margaret, in 1960, Karl assumed the post of executive director of the Afro-Anglo-American Program for Teacher Education in Africa (AAA), funded by the Carnegie Corporation of New York, and embracing a membership of the University of London's Institute of Education, Department of Education in Tropical Areas; Teachers College; and six Sub-Saharan African institutes or faculties of education in East, Southern, and West Africa. During the period 1960–1969, Karl nurtured his "second love" into an organization that included more than thirty African member institutions before the executive offices were most appropriately transferred to Africa in 1969.

In addition to his duties with the AAA Program at Teachers College, for several years he was director of the newly constituted Institute for Education in Africa, which coordinated African research and training activities, including the Teachers for East Africa (TEA) and, later, the Teacher Education for East Africa (TEEA) programs, plus Peace Corps training programs for secondary school teachers for East and West Africa. Directly or indirectly, as program director or consultant, during the decade 1961–1971, Karl was active in the training of nearly 2,500 Americans at Teachers College for service as secondary school teachers or teacher training college tutors in Africa.

As vice-chairman of the Overseas Liaison Committee of the American Council on Education, Karl had many commitments to assist institutions of higher education in Africa, most notably in his role as member of the Provisional Council and Council of the University of Zambia, 1964–1973.

THE ADVISER

In 1937 Karl served as consultant on social studies for the General Education Board. Later he served as consultant/director for several UNESCO seminars on education in Europe.

From 1960–1969 he served as consultant to the TEA and TEEA programs at Teachers College. After his service as member and vice-chairman of the Overseas Liaison Committee, he served for several years as consultant to that organization.

His most gratifying consultancy was that with the Association for Teacher Education in Africa (ATEA) after the offices moved from Teachers College to Africa. Until 1976 this kept him in touch with all the individuals and institutions with whom he had been working since 1960.

All in all, Karl Bigelow served fifty-six years as professor, administrator, and consultant for institutions in America, Europe, and Africa.

THE MAN

Karl Bigelow was the prime example of the professor who truly loved to teach. His courses at Teachers College were always over-subscribed due to his superb talents as a lecturer, his infectious enthusiasm, and his involvement of students in the process.

Given the length of his career, the list of scholarly research and publications he produced is rather limited. However, he devoted his time to teaching others the art as exemplified by the numerous dissertations and other books of his students on his office bookshelves.

His zest for life and his breadth of interests seemed boundless. He was a devotee of the ballet and, in earlier years, was the caller for Saturday night square dances during the summers in Temple, New Hampshire. He was an inveterate reader on an unlimited range of topics. During his latter years he became a student of gourmet cooking and the cookware involved, resulting in numerous trips to Zabar's and Bridge Company, food and kitchenware specialty shops in Manhattan. Karl was also addicted to gadgetry, seeming always to be the first to purchase the latest gimmick for home or office.

The man was equally at ease with a head of state or the elevator operator in the halls of Teachers College. He had a genuine interest in the welfare and activities of all those with whom he had contact. Perhaps one of his greatest qualities was to give the impression that in any conversation what one was saying was the most important thing in life to Karl Bigelow at that given moment.

While most understanding, kind, and tolerant, Karl had certain standards. His equilibrium was upset if his standards were not maintained. He could not tolerate poor service, loud music, or mediocre wines in a restaurant. Shoddy writing and shallow thinking were rejected out-of-hand. Lack of punctuality for appointments or delay in opening conference sessions were always painful. Also, ineffective administrative and budgetary practices brought forth reams of corrective notes. One of his greatest compliments as consultant to ATEA was paid by an African officer of the organization who said, "Whenever I received a letter from Karl Bigelow in New York, I told my secretary, 'Do not open this letter until I have had two stiff drinks and a good dinner!' "

Karl's enthusiasm for the latest of four or five books he might have read during the week was not always equally shared by his relatives or close friends who had to sit through lengthy verbal reviews of the tome during lunch or dinner. The delightful fact was that he was so engrossed in the telling that he never realized that it might be boring to the listener.

A fitting conclusion to these recollections of this great human being is Karl's version of a conversation with a Nigerian lady at his latest ATEA conference dinner at Ibadan in 1976, when he was specially honored for his contributions to African teacher education. His banquet companion asked, "Dr. Bigelow, how did you become interested in African education?" Karl responded, "Do you really want to know the whole story?" and launched into thirty minutes or so of exposition. Upon concluding, he asked, "Now aren't you sorry you raised the question?" Whereupon the Nigerian lady replied, "Dr. Bigelow, I had been told that you were long-winded, but you are certainly most interesting!" Later, on telling the story, Karl exclaimed, "I want that statement for my epitaph!"

To know this man was sheer joy.

Karl W. Bigelow, (Grand) Father of ATEA: Tribute to a Great Educator and Humanist

A. BABATUNDE FAFUNWA

University of Ife, Nigeria

When I was asked by the president of the Association for Teacher Education in Africa, Professor Newman Smart, to propose the toast to Professor Karl Bigelow on the occasion of his retirement from the ATEA, I felt like the man who was introducing a great personality of world renown. The poor man went on extolling the qualities of his subject, but his audience was growing impatient. At a point the audience shouted in annoyance, "We know the man, but who are you?"

A couple of years ago I was asked to pay a tribute to Professor Freeman Butts and I said *inter alia* that Freeman Butts could not fill Karl Bigelow's shoes; no one could anyway. So Freeman Butts designed his own shoes and filled them admirably.

Karl Bigelow was a remarkable, vivacious Africanist and humanist. Karl stood tall and erect as an Africanist even at the time when it was not fashionable to be an Africanist cum educator in or out of Africa. Karl had abiding faith in African education and African capabilities.

I first met Karl at the University of Nigeria, Nsukka, in 1961 at a conference convened by the authorities of that university to discuss an African university curriculum for teacher education. Karl became my instant hero from that day on. We met at various conferences at least every other year from 1961–1977 and he never let me down. Karl was a tower of strength in the 1960s and was still going strong in the 1970s.

Karl was a durable fellow, as all ATEA brethren know. He outlasted the original co-founders of the Afro-Anglo-American Program

(AAA)—Professors L. J. Lewis and Andy Taylor—both of whom discovered new pastures in the United Kingdom. Karl shook hands with General Amin in 1971, the emperor of Ethiopia in 1972, and General Gowon in 1973, all in the interests of ATEA!

Karl will be long remembered by all AAA/ATEA members as:

The grandsire of ATEA.

A stickler for details, particularly about Carnegie grants and budgets!

Hail fellow well met, even at eighty! Karl's jokes and witty remarks could fill a book or two. His jokes inspired all of us to seek ways and means of topping them, but only a few like Steve Stackpole, Carl Manone, and Sentenza Kajubi succeeded, not in outclassing Karl's, but in making the rest of us smile! ATEA members are hard to please, but Karl rocked them more than most!

Once, at the University of Cape Coast in Ghana, Asiedu-Akrofi and others insisted that the oldest member (age-wise) of the ATEA must pour libation. Karl was the obvious choice, but Karl loved his whisky and soda in those days. Characteristically, Karl, who was economy-minded about everything, insisted that if he must give part of his drinks to the gods, someone must first guarantee him a refill!

Was it not Professor Nick Anim of Ghana who once said: "Karl is the only one I know who can sleep with his eyes open"? The truth is that Karl, unlike many of us, could sit through a long session without dozing off at any time. He always wanted to be sure that he did not miss a thing!

I have no talent for poetic verses, but thinking about Karl's impending departure from the ATEA inspired the following and I am speaking it as it occurred to me:

That Karl Bigelow
Is really a big fellow.
He's as tall as he's big;
He straddles the educational
    horizon of Africa
Like a colossus,
Waging war against
    ignorance and darkness
    in Teacher Education.

He was later joined by
    younger ATEA-ers
To whom he bestows his attires
For battles yet to be won.
May his shadow never grow less,
May his fellowship with ATEA
    be everlasting,
Through Karl Bigelow Lectures
    and permanent life membership
    of ATEA.
To a great man called Bigelow
We say a Big Hello.
Let's rise to toast this
    Karl, Big Fellow!

An Appreciation
of Professor Karl W. Bigelow

W. A. DODD

*Formerly Adviser in Education
to the Overseas Development Agency
of Her Majesty's United Kingdom Government*

When in March, 1980, Professor Karl Bigelow lay dying, and knew that he was, he called for his friend and former assistant, Carl Graham, and addressed him in these terms: "I want you to go down to the *New York Times* Office; bring back the draft of my obituary; and I shall correct it, for this is one goddam thing the *New York Times* is going to get right." And those words echoed in my mind as I prepared this brief appreciation of a wonderful character who lived with style and left life in style.

First, a word about his renown as a lecturer and teacher at Teachers College, Columbia University, New York, where he flourished between 1945 and 1963. You will have noticed that I said "lecturer and *teacher*," and not "lecturer and researcher," not "lecturer and writer." This was deliberate because above all Karl Bigelow was a teacher and teacher trainer; he was not a "publish or perish" man. Most of Karl Bigelow's British friends know little about this career. However, they would not be surprised to know that his lectures on the history of American education drew large student audiences, attracted as much as anything by the professor's gift for illustrative anecdote. One such anecdote was retold to me. It concerned the arrival of a new reforming president at Teachers College who, in the face of opposition from the dean, introduced the system whereby students were allowed to choose for themselves the course and combination of courses they followed. At the beginning of the experiment, and during the week of registration, the dean stopped one student and asked him what courses he had chosen. The dean was astonished when the student indicated a most impressively balanced and imaginative mixture of major and minor courses, arts and sciences, practical and theoretical. Marveling, the dean asked the student what criteria he had used to make such a perfect selection. The student replied, "Well, I decided to go to no classes before 10:30 A.M. and no classes after 4 P.M., to go to no classes above the fifth floor, to go to no classes given by women. And that's how it worked out."

Another point about this phase of Karl Bigelow's career is that out of his interest in the history of education in America, in the role of education as a means of development for the blacks of the southern states in the period of Reconstruction in the Jeanes schools, in the Hampton Institute, in the fund established by Caroline Phelps-Stokes, out of all this, in large measure, stemmed his interest in education in Africa.

I turn, therefore, to his second career, the career which led to his close involvement with education and in particular teacher education in what were the former British colonies in tropical Africa. In a way it began, I suppose, with the conference at Teachers College which he held for educators from Africa in 1949. His pioneering interest developed further when in 1952 he toured eastern, southern, central, and west Africa on a tour sponsored by the Institute of Education and the then British Colonial Office. It developed even further when in 1960 the Afro-Anglo-American Program for Teacher Education in Africa (AAA) was founded, after which, with the involvement of such figures as John Lewis, Andy Taylor, Sir Christopher Cox, and others, teacher education and in particular teacher education at the university level in Africa grew remarkably. These were the years of the Association for Teacher Education in Africa (ATEA). These were the years of the Teachers for East Africa (TEA) and Teacher Education for East Africa (TEEA) schemes. In that period from 1960 to his death in 1980, Karl Bigelow was a regular traveler to Africa, a welcome visitor and a friend to so many key African figures in education at that time. So regular a visitor was he, indeed, that his favorite drink, a dry martini on the rocks with a twist of lemon, became known in many a hotel as a "Bigelow"; and there was a time when you could walk into the Norfolk Hotel in Nairobi, the New Africa Hotel in Dar es Salaam, or the Ridgeway Hotel in Lusaka and order a "Bigelow" and the bar steward would respond with a knowing smile.

If Karl Bigelow's involvement with Africa over a period of almost thirty years was rich and bountiful, so also was his link with the United Kingdom. That began, as I understand, with his early sponsorship by the Institute of Education, University of London, and his attendance at the historic Cambridge conference of 1952 on education in British tropical Africa. It grew when he came to the Institute in 1958 as a visiting lecturer. Once the Afro-Anglo-American Program was established in 1960, he was a regular visitor to London. Never a year went by when he did not visit London at least once, and more often several times. Perhaps there was no more touching testimony to his affection for London and this institute than his attendance in 1977 at the fiftieth anniversary celebrations of what is now called the Department of Education in Developing Countries. His understanding of the British and his love for the British, were alike, deep. One of his favorite remarks, I recall, was that when he was faced with a crisis, when everything was going wrong, when his whole program was crumbling around him, he used to say to himself: "Now what would the British do in these circumstances?" and, as he said, "I would decide that in these circumstances the British would do absolutely *nothing*; and that is precisely what I would do."

But for all his fame in education, for all his work for Africa and with UNESCO, Karl Bigelow will also be remembered as a raconteur, as a *bon viveur*, as a master of the appropriate anecdote. There are many anecdotes one might tell that epitomize his sense of humour. Let me choose just one. I was present in New York in Teachers College on his seventieth birthday in 1969; there were but three of us in his office and, knowing that it was his birthday, one of us produced a bottle of sherry and four glasses and we drank a toast to Karl Bigelow. Jocularly I cried, "Speech," and with typical urbanity Karl Bigelow replied: "I recall the story of that famous American justice, Oliver Wendell Holmes, who on his *ninetieth* birthday was walking down Independence Avenue, Washington, on a fine spring day; it was lunchtime and out of the offices of Washington poured dozens of pretty young American girls, looking their most attractive. And on his ninetieth birthday Wendell Holmes turned to his colleagues and said, 'My God, I wish I were *seventy* again.' "

Well there it is. There we have Karl Bigelow—raconteur, lecturer, friend of Africa and African education, and friend of this institute and this country. Perhaps I have understated the case. Perhaps I should have painted Karl Bigelow in rather more glowing colors, but I doubt whether he would have liked that. Once in 1969 I was introducing him to a group of young Americans who, in the Teacher Education for East Africa Program, were preparing to go out to Kenya, Uganda, and Tanzania; as I went forward to introduce him to his audience, Karl Bigelow whispered to me, "For God's sake don't drown me in sweet maple syrup." And if Karl Bigelow is listening tonight, I hope that he will agree that I haven't done that.

At any rate, just as he corrected his own obituary for the *New York Times*, so he chose his own epitaph. It stemmed from a conversation with a Nigerian lady whom he met at the last conference dinner of the Association for Teacher Education in Africa. His neighbor at table asked him, "Dr. Bigelow, how did you become interested in African education?" And he launched into a thirty-minute reply. At the conclusion he said, "Now, aren't you sorry that you asked that question?" Whereupon the lady from Nigeria said, "Dr. Bigelow, I had been told that you were long-winded, but you were also most interesting." Thereafter, in telling the story, Karl Bigelow always added with a chuckle, "I want *that* for my epitaph." And so let it be.

THE
MEMORIAL
LECTURES

Higher Education and the Dilemma of Nation-Building in Africa: A Retrospective and Prospective View

W. SENTEZA KAJUBI

National Institute of Education
Makerere University, Kampala, Uganda

John Dewey said in the foreword of a book published in 1919, after his visit to Japan, that anyone who has enjoyed the unique hospitality of Japan will be overwhelmed with confusion if he endeavors to make an acknowledgment in any way commensurate to the kindness he received.

It is a privilege and a great honor for me to be called upon to deliver the first in a series of lectures dedicated to the late Karl Worth Bigelow, formerly Professor Emeritus at Teachers College, Columbia University, in remembrance and recognition of his many years of exceptional and devoted efforts dedicated to the study and promotion of higher and teacher education in general, and particularly in Africa. But at the same time let me say that, like John Dewey, anyone who has enjoyed or witnessed the unique fellowship of the Afro-Anglo-American Program for Teacher Education in Africa (AAA), the dynamic leadership of Teachers College in the field of international education, and the generosity and "creative philanthropy" of the Carnegie Corporation of New York toward education, would be overwhelmed with confusion if he tried to give an account in any way commensurate with the impressive and all-pervading contribution which Karl Bigelow and, through

---

Lecture delivered on January 28, 1982, at Teachers College, Columbia University.

him, the Carnegie Corporation and Teachers College made to the development of education in the early stages of nation-building in Africa. Professor Bigelow saw investment in education as the most productive means of effecting a smooth transition from colonial status to independence in the emergent states of Africa. The expansion of higher education and the improvement of the education of teachers were to him vital links in the process of nation-building. For a period which spanned over three decades, but particularly from the 1960s, Professor Bigelow was deeply involved in the internationalization of concern for the development of education in Africa: he was instrumental in the formation of the African Liaison Committee, which later became the Overseas Liaison Committee of the American Council on Education. It was largely through his initiative that the Afro-Anglo-American Program for cooperation in teacher education and the Teachers for East Africa (TEA) scheme were inaugurated. All these endeavors and many others in which Karl Bigelow was the chief engineer, Teachers College, the engine driver, and the Carnegie Corporation of New York, the stoker or generator, helped to move the train of African education through a crucial period of unprecedented change in the history of the continent. It was not by accident, therefore, that Karl Bigelow was honored by several universities in Africa and was cited by Teachers College, Columbia University, as "pedagogical bridge builder, gentle and precise interpreter of different cultures, instructive inspector of traditions . . . and prominent teacher of teachers."[1]

All of Africa has been liberated, with the exception of Namibia and Azania (South Africa); and those countries which became independent in the early 1960s have now reached the age of maturity. Since a fundamental goal of education, particularly higher education, is to promote national integration and economic and social development, it is appropriate, after two decades of independence, to have a Janus look at the role of higher education in nation-building in Africa.

This paper is mainly an examination of the progress that African universities are making in their search for relevance toward nation-building, and the problems they are facing in trying to accomplish this task. While no ready-made solutions are available to the many intractable problems concerning education and African development, a number of questions are raised and suggestions made for possible future directions in higher education in Africa.

EDUCATION AND SOCIETY IN AFRICA

According to an old saying of the Western Sudan, "Salt [was] from the north, gold from the south and silver from the White man's country, but the word of God and the treasures of wisdom [were] to be found in Timbuktu." The story further goes that the sons of Songhai Kings quitted their palaces in Gao, and the children of the Tuaregs and Moors deserted their great tents in order to go to Sankore, where the famous Mohamed ben Abou Bekr, more than one thousand years ago gave lectures and said prayers from dawn to dusk.[2] The noted scholar Leo Africanus in describing Timbuktu as it was during the mid-fifteenth century wrote: "There are numerous judges, doctors and clerics, all receiving good salaries from the King. He pays great respect to the men of learning. There is a big demand for books in manuscript, imported from Barbary. More profit is made from the book trade than from any other business."[3]

The moral of the story is to explode the myth and dispel the view which is unfortunately still held in some circles that there was no civilization, no history, let alone organized education until the advent of white missionaries in precolonial Africa.

Plato in his treatise on education, *The Republic*, as paraphrased by Lawrence Cremin, argues that "in order to talk about the good life, we have to talk about the good society, and in order to talk about the good society, we have to talk about the kind of education that will bring that society into existence and sustain it."[4] In other words, according to Plato, there is a universal dialectical relationship between education and society. There is no image of society that does not assume a particular type of education and conversely every type of education implies or subsumes an image of man and society. This was true in precolonial Africa as it is everywhere today. Every tribe, clan, or nation evolved its own distinctive culture and an education system to sustain it, based on the life of the community and its environment.

Generally, there were no school buildings as such, and no specialized teachers like Mohamed ben Abou Bekr, but in every African society there was and there still is a curriculum—an embodiment of skills, social practices, customs, symbols, rituals, values, and attitudes which individuals must learn according to their age and sex. Education was conceived as a living process linked to the daily experience of every individual. People learned by doing meaningful things; the homestead or the village was the school;[5] and everyone was in one way or another a learner, a teacher, and a worker. When the long day's work was done and the mothers were preparing the evening meal, the grandparents kept the children awake and spellbound with fireside stories, puzzles, and riddles. Through these stories in which the hare outwits the elephant, the leopard, and the lion, the tortoise wins the race against the hare, and the termites cooperatively build their anthill, the children learned that wisdom is more valuable than physical strength and that humility is more to be prized than ostentatiousness. They also learned that cooperation is strength and division, weakness. Good should be rewarded and evil punished.

When viewed in retrospect, as David Scanlon points out, the African traditional curriculum provided a well-rounded and integrated education:

> Here the theory was combined with the practical. The bush school (meaning the Poro and Sandi Societies of the Mendi people of Sierra Leone) was an opportunity for apprentices to be trained in craft skills. They learned the history and laws of their people. Boys who graduated together were considered "brothers" bound for life in a close relationship . . . values were established and for the young men and women, laws governing every aspect of daily living were learned.[6]

Thus, in every generation, as Jomo Kenyatta says of the Kikuyu, the tribal organization is established and knit together by the activities of various age groups of old and young people who act harmoniously, in the political, social, religious and economic life of the tribe.[7] It is not intended here to glamorize or romanticize the past and advocate a return to bygone days, but only to say that there is much that modern formal education can and should draw from the philosophy and practices of traditional education. These practices are generally lacking in the education imparted by formal schooling in Africa today. Traditional African education sought first and foremost to instill values and skills of community life and mutual cooperation or "vital participation" as Vincent Mulago[8] calls it, and, in the words of Kofi Busia, to produce leaders and ordinary men and women "who put the interests of the group above their personal interests; whose ears are warm towards the members of their family and kinfolk; who dutifully fulfilled obligations hallowed and approved by tradition, out of reverence for ancestors and gods."[9]

It was this type of education and variations in it which made one Mende, Hausa, Yoruba, or Ibo; Ashanti, Fanti, or Ewe; Masai, Luo, or Kikuyu; and Muganda, Acholi, or Karamojong.

Universities are also not completely new to Africa. They have a long and venerable record in the history of the continent. Life institutes which specialized in religion and medicine, that are said to have had the character of universities, existed in ancient Egypt.[10] Universities such as Sankore in Timbuktu (now defunct) where Mohamed ben Abou Bekr taught, Al Azhar in Cairo, and Qurawalzine in Fez, Morocco, were long in existence before some of the oldest universities in Europe and North America were established. Indeed, taken in sum as Victor Ferkiss points out, in the mid-fifteenth century "the culture and political organization of the Sudanic states was comparable to that of Spain and more developed than that of the ruder northern parts of Europe."[11]

HIGHER EDUCATION AND THE MANPOWER CRISIS

In spite of the ancient roots of education in Africa, schools and universities as we know them today are a phenomenon of very recent times. By the end of 1950, for example, the whole of sub-Saharan Africa produced only 8,000 secondary school graduates, 40 percent of whom were in two countries—Ghana and Nigeria. By 1958 there were less than 10,000 African students in institutions of higher learning both at home and abroad, and 6,500 of them or 65 percent were from Nigeria and Ghana.[12] Most African universities of today were not established before 1960. The shortage of indigenous high-level and middle-level manpower, or human capital, prior to independence was therefore a crucial problem in all African countries.

It was the realization of this incipient manpower crisis by concerned individuals of good will and by philanthropic organizations in the United States that gave rise to a series of vital conferences about African education prior to and during 1960. In May, 1958, for example, representatives of governments, universities, and foundations from the United States and England met at the Greenbrier Hotel in White Sulphur Springs, West Virginia, and agreed to assist African higher education. It has been mainly the "Greenbrier spirit" that has maintained an active interest in African education to date.[13] The Ashby Commission on Post-School Certificate and Higher Education in Nigeria was appointed in April, 1959, and presented its historic report entitled *Investment in Education* in September, 1960. In the same year a conference on education in East Africa was held at Princeton University. This resulted in the launching of the Teachers for East Africa Project to strengthen the supply of secondary school teachers for Kenya, Tanzania, and Uganda. The year 1960 also saw the inauguration of the Afro-Anglo-American Program in which Teachers College, Columbia University, the University of London Institute of Education, and institutes and departments of education in Anglophone Africa would cooperate in the improvement of the quality of education for teachers. It is significant to point out that most, if not all, of these conferences were organized with Karl Bigelow and Teachers College in the background and with the moral and financial support of the Carnegie Corporation of New York.

In discussing the development of education in Africa, it is impossible to escape mention of the political significance of the year 1960. The year 1960 has been referred to as the year of Africa and Africa's Year of Independence. Within that year alone seventeen African countries gained their independence, and thirteen others were to become independent states a few years later. The sudden collapse of the edifice of colonialism and the emergence of the "political kingdom" triggered even greater expectations and demands not only for the total elimination of the vestiges of foreign rule from the rest of the continent, but also for the liberation of the masses of the people from disease, poverty, and ignorance. Harold Macmillan's wind of change and Frederick Harbison's revolution of rising expectations had begun to sweep across the continent.

The 1960s were characterized at the same time by an unprecedented emphasis on development and by great faith and enthusiasm placed in the power of education as a lever of national development. The United Nations dedicated the years 1960–1970 as the Development Decade during which concerted efforts would be made "to lessen the gap, to speed up the process of modernization, to release the majority of mankind from crippling poverty, to mitigate the tensions and hostilities, which must flow from the world's vast inequalities in wealth."[14] Economists and other social scientists had also just discovered close linkages or reciprocal relationships between education and development. Education systems would produce people with the knowledge, skills, and attitudes and values that not only were favorable to economic and social development but were a sine qua non for the process of national integration.

"The building of modern nations," wrote Harbison and Myers, "depends upon the development of people and the organization of human activity. Capital, natural resources, foreign aid, and international trade, of course, play important roles in economic growth, but none is more important than manpower." Indeed, they pointed out, "If a country is unable to develop its human resources, it cannot build anything else, whether it be a modern political system, a sense of national unity, or a prosperous economy."[15]

African states also saw their systems of formal education as a principal if not the chief means of achieving economic and social development and guaranteeing the benefits of the newly hard-won independence. The Conference of Ministers of Education of Independent States in Africa, held in Addis Ababa in 1961, declared: "The citizens of Africa see in Education a means by which their aspirations may be met. They are willing to sacrifice for the attainment of this means for gaining economic and social development and wish to provide for more and more of their people education suited to their desires."[16]

The Addis Ababa conference was a significant milestone in the development of education in Africa. It was the first international conference to be called on the continent to discuss education not only *for* but also *by* Africans themselves. It launched the new development philosophy based on the recognition that the entire educational system, and in particular higher education, plays a pivotal role in the social, economic, and cultural transformation of nations. The optimism, enthusiasm, and political resolve which the ministers had at the time are reflected in the ambitious targets they set for themselves to be achieved by the year 1980. They envisaged: (1) free compulsory universal primary education (UPE); (2) education at the secondary level to be provided to 30 percent of the candidates who complete primary school; (3) higher education to be provided mostly in Africa to 20 percent of those who complete secondary education; and (4) the improvement of the quality of African schools and universities as a constant aim.[17]

A year later, in 1962, the education ministers met again, this time in Tananarive (now Antananarivo), Madagascar, to draw up a master plan for the development of higher education in Africa. At this conference African universities were assigned seven roles:

To teach and advance knowledge through research
To maintain adherence and loyalty to world academic standards
To ensure unification of Africa
To encourage elucidation of and appreciation for African culture
    and heritage and to dispel misconceptions about Africa, through
    research and teaching of African studies
To train the "whole man" for nation-building
To develop human resources for meeting manpower needs
To evolve over the years truly African institutions for higher learn-
    ing dedicated to Africa and its people, yet promoting a bond of
    kinship to the larger human society

The expansion of science and technology received special emphasis, and
it was recommended that the proportion of all African students enrolled
in scientific and technological subjects including medicine and agriculture should reach not less than 60 percent by 1980.[18]

The faith which national leaders have in higher education to bring
about national development is further indicated by the fact that most
university acts in Africa designate the presidents as the chancellors or
heads of their national universities. Julius Nyerere referred to university
people as the "torch bearers of our society and the protectors of the
flame," and Kwame Nkrumah, the first president of Ghana, saw the
university as "the Academic focus of national life, reflecting the social,
economic, cultural, and political aspirations of the people."[19] African
universities are thus seen as the main vehicles of nation-building. They
are, as the ministers concluded at Tananarive, at once the main instruments of national progress, the chief guardians of the people's heritage,
and the voice of the people in international councils of technology and
scholarship.

In addition to the foregoing general objectives, African universities
have been progressively expected by governments and the public at large
to play a major and increasing role in development tasks. They are expected to serve national policy and public welfare in "direct, immediate
and practical ways."[20]

PROGRESS SINCE 1960

To what extent, then, have the expectations and the efforts of
African leaders and philanthropic organizations through investment in

education, particularly higher education, come to fruition? There is no doubt that the growth of universities and colleges of higher education in Africa has resulted in the output of young men and women trained at different levels of competence in various fields. This expansion has quickened the Africanization of the civil services and the private sectors. Key technical and managerial positions formerly held by foreigners are now occupied by Africans.

Education systems in general and health services have also been considerably expanded. The percentage of children of primary school age has more than doubled, while the growth of secondary and higher education has surpassed the Addis Ababa expectations. Infant mortality rates have been lowered and life expectancy raised in all African countries. Epidemics such as smallpox or typhoid have virtually been eliminated, and locusts and other pests which used to periodically destroy hundreds of thousands of acres of croplands have also been brought under control. Engineering feats such as the Volta River Dam, Tema Harbor, the Tanzam Railway, and many miles of modern highways have been accomplished, albeit with external technical assistance. National philosophies or ideologies purveying different versions of African democracy, such as Ujamaa, humanism, negritude, Nyayo, authenticity, and many others have emerged in the last twenty years. Freedom fighters for total African liberation have triumphed in Mozambique, Angola, and Zimbabwe, and the struggle continues in Namibia and Azania.

SLOW PROGRESS

But when all is said and done, the picture that African countries project over the last two decades is grim. It is one of slow, nagging, and in many cases negative economic, social, and political development amounting to what can be called a real continental crisis. Despite fantastic and almost heroic expansions in school and university enrollments, there are still crippling shortages of high-level manpower, and the number of students in higher education compared to the relevant age groups is still woefully small.

Universal primary education (UPE) envisaged for 1980 for the whole of Africa is far from being a reality, and is likely to remain on the agenda of several countries even beyond the year 2000. Moreover, of all the children who enter primary education, over 50 percent do not complete the cycle, and the dropout rate between grade one and grade two is as high as 40 percent for some countries. Even those who complete the primary cycle contain 70 percent who fail to continue on to secondary school for lack of adequate provision. There are yawning gaps between the enrollments of males and those of females, particularly in higher education, and great discrepancies in the provision of social amenities between urban and rural areas. Adult literacy rates hardly exceed 30 percent in most countries and in some countries are still as low as only 5 to 10 percent.

Although life expectancy at birth has improved somewhat from thirty-nine years in 1960 to forty-seven years in 1979 and infant mortality rates lowered considerably, death rates in Africa are still by far the highest in the world, and out of every one hundred babies born to African mothers, fifteen to twenty do not see their first birthday.

Although Africa is politely or euphemistically referred to as a "developing region," paradoxically nowhere, with the embarrassing exception of South Africa, can the continent be said to be really developing. Of the thirty-eight countries described by the World Bank in 1981 as low-income countries (with per capita incomes less than $340 per year), twenty-four or 63 percent are in Africa, and of the thirty countries identified by the United Nations Conference on Trade and Development (UN CTAD) as the poorest in the world, twenty are in Africa. Of the thirty-nine sub-Saharan countries surveyed by the World Bank in 1979, only fifteen recorded annual economic growth rates of more than 2 percent between 1960 and 1979; and eight countries, including two Afro-Anglo-American Program (AAA)/Association for Teacher Education in Africa (ATEA) members—Ghana and Uganda—experienced negative rates of growth.[21]

The desire of African governments to foster agricultural development through education has not yet been anywhere realized. Hidden curricula, public economic and social reward systems heavily weighted in favor of urban life, and nonmanual skills are everywhere pulling the young people toward towns and preventing the benefits of education from being recycled into rural development. Average annual growth rates in the volume of food production have risen only slightly while the population has been growing at the rapid rate of 2.8 to 3 percent per annum. The net result is that per capita food production has decreased in most African countries to levels below those of 1960. Malnutrition, kwashiorkor, and periodic starvation are endemic all over Africa. Indeed, it would not be an exaggeration, although it would be funny if it were not true, to say that the dogs and cats in the United States are fed much better than the people in Africa, with the exception of the lucky few. All sub-Saharan countries have depended in one way or another on food aid imports, despite the fact that most of these countries have vast areas of virgin arable lands.

Civil and military strife, sporadic guerrilla warfare, subversion from outside and from within the countries and the continent, interethnic and religious rivalry, and fragile political infrastructures of all types are endemic in most countries of the subcontinent. Between January, 1963, and January, 1982, Africa experienced over forty-five military coups d'etat, and Ghana, the first African country to gain independence and therefore the torch bearer of African liberation, has led the way with five coups between February, 1966, and January, 1982. Samuel Decalo, who has made a thorough study of these coups, including their motives, concluded that there was little if any evidence "beyond rhetoric and pious declarations of any sincere desire by most of the military regimes in tropical Africa to bring about fundamental social change or rearrange the structure of power within African states."[22] In other words, the incessant and in many ways insensate coups, one can only conclude, are mainly due to intrigue and greed for personal power. This political instability must be in a large measure responsible for Africa's economic, social, and cultural stagnation or retardation. The coups d'etat have often been accompanied by mass arrests, detentions without trial, public firing squads or hangings, massacres, and sometimes almost complete decimation of certain ethnic groups, and in all cases by severe curtailment or total elimination of fundamental human rights and freedoms, such as freedom of assembly and freedom of thought and expression. As yet relatively few African countries have ratified the International Covenant on Civil and Political Rights and similar international instruments.

In this situation the universities have had a largely teaching role, concentrating of necessity and until recently on the undergraduate role, and being the offspring largely of the Western tradition greatly affected by the content and practice of the United Kingdom, United States, and French universities. Increasingly, though slowly, they are gaining confidence in relating their teaching and research activities to the practical basic problems of national development. Above all, universities have been criticized for their tendency to foster careerism, aloofness, and ivory-towerism in their graduates, thereby failing to produce men and women who are prime movers of development. Higher education has been conceived too much in terms of satisfying manpower needs per se, that is, in terms of what the graduates are going *to do*, rather than what sort of people they are going *to be*. There are popular opinions to the effect that very often school, college, and university graduates lack the necessary motivation and dedication for duty. Education has filled them with great awareness of their *rights* and *entitlements*, but has failed to kindle in them to the same extent the *sense of duty and responsibility*. There is widespread lamentation about the apparent failure of our graduates in this respect. Eni Njoku, for example, as vice-chancellor of the University of Nigeria, Nsukka, had occasion to point out:

> In spite of the availability of highly educated people in positions of leadership, problems of social integration are as acute as ever, neither governments animated by principles of parliamentary democracy nor those motivated by specific ideologies have prospered, neither private nor public business enterprise has succeeded to levels required to support a modern nation; corruption and lack of public responsibility have afflicted the educated and uneducated alike. There is therefore a great disillusionment about the role of education. Either the type of university education offered up to now has been inadequate, or the number of educated has been too small to make the necessary impact.[23]

S. O. Biobaku, another vice-chancellor, complained: "Our intellectuals wallow in the same morass of false living, unbecoming display of wealth and conspicuous consumption as do the uneducated. We [intellectuals] do not come clean from the charges of nepotism, bribery and corruption."[24]

Throughout Africa, the people are getting impatient with the slow pace of development and with the maldistribution of social and economic progress. For example, in Sierra Leone, which is not atypical, the distribution of incomes is so heavily skewed that just 6 percent of the population take home over one-third of the national income, and it is this group whose incomes are increasing fastest.[25] The preindependence slogans of "seek ye first the political kingdom, and the rest will be added upon you" and other appeals to the emotion of the masses have proved false and can no longer be taken as a substitute for real progress. The experience of the last two decades seems to suggest that even the little that the people had is being taken away. Titles of such books as *Not Yet Uhuru* by a former vice-president of an African country, *State of Blood* by a former minister of justice of another African country, and *Africa Strangled* by a perceptive external observer seem to suggest that the "revolution of rising aspirations" is turning into a revolution of rising frustrations. Okot p'Bitek of Uganda laments the situation with a verse in the "Song of Lowino":

> And those who have
> Fallen into things
> Throw themselves into soft beds
> But the hip bones of the voters
> Grow painful
> Sleeping on the same (bare) earth
> They slept
> Before Uhuru.

"Uhuru," concludes p'Bitek, "actually means the replacement of foreign rule by native dictatorships—by those trained in our own schools and universities."[26]

Perhaps the enthusiasm and the aftermath of new independence and the romantic view of the 1960s toward the power of education, led African leaders and the world at large to place too many items on the development agenda that education, let alone formal education acting by itself, could not and cannot accomplish. It is true, however, that it is still toward education that the people look for solving the basic problems of life. As Ferkiss wrote: "Education is the fulcrum by means of which leaders expect to create the new Africa, as well as the focus of the humble villager hoping for a better life for his children."[27] President Siaka Stevens of Sierra Leone has referred to education as "All Our Future." It is through the library stacks rather than through the barracks that Africa hopes to go furthest in her search for the "ideal of man"[28] and for a new identity.

Each society, according to Durkheim, forms its own "ideal of man,"[29] and it is this image of man that forms or should form the focus of the education system. What is the ideal of man in a continent fraught with political turmoil and social upheavals, in which the most important cultural activity is to keep alive?

Shakespeare's Hamlet was faced with the dilemma of choosing between whether to suffer the "slings and arrows of outrageous fortune, or to take arms against a sea of troubles, and by opposing, end them."[30]

Higher education in Africa faces a similar dilemma in its search for the ideal of man. A given education system can either act as a mirror and reflect—or reproduce—the existing society with all its social ills and political woes or contribute to changing them by striving to produce better human beings. But what is a "good or better man"? "Is he," as Edgar Castle asked, "the prototype of Plato's pupil 'Who passionately desires to become a perfect citizen, knowing how to rule and how to be ruled on the basis of (truth) and justice'?; or is he the 'go-getter' reaping where he has not sown, or the man who neither reaps nor sows?"[31] What type of education will provide the necessary skills for rapid industrialization and rural development and at the same time provide the social and political mobilization for national integration? Should we accept and adapt ourselves to all that Western education and technology can offer or should we try to extract from foreign textbooks and foreign teachers the needed skills and leave out the ideological framework and hidden values which denigrate indigenous cultures?

On the other hand, real education is, to use Edmund Stillman's words, a "subversive" activity. It should make people critically conscious in that they become not just recipients of information, but knowing subjects with a "deepening awareness both of the socio-cultural reality which shapes their lives and of their capacity to transform that reality."[32] How many teachers and leaders in Africa today would like students and masses who are critically conscious? How many African leaders would genuinely join Julius Nyerere in saying: "We need people with suggestions who are not afraid to speak their mind"?[33] I do not have the wisdom of King Solomon or the problem-solving mind of Socrates to answer these questions concisely here and now. But one thing seems clear to me and that is that national leaders as well as all those who are concerned with education at all levels cannot escape the moral responsibility of asking the questions as to what is a good man, and what sort of men and women we would like to create. For Africa today whether to change or not to change the current patterns of life is not the question. Change is not merely a choice; it is an absolute necessity if Africa is not going to limp or crawl behind the rest of the world for eternity, and to continue to feed her people on the crumbs from the white man's table. Another

development, as economists say these days, requires another e
if new patterns of development are going to evolve.[34]

THE CRISIS OF NATIONAL INTEGRATION

A major problem regarding educational and social reform in Africa
is the lack in most countries on the continent of a national ethos or
philosophy around which to coil the education system and to bring the
people together into a social order with a collective common purpose.
Poverty, ignorance, and disease are frequently given as the major problems of Africa and as the main indices of underdevelopment. This is
true but only partly so. Poverty, disease, and ignorance are only symp-
toms and not the real causes of African underdevelopment. At the tap-
root of Africa's underdevelopment is the lack of national unity and
cohesion. The problems of development are mainly social rather than
physical. African countries are poor not because they lack natural resources
such as minerals, arable land, reliable rainfall, forests, and lakes. African
poverty and social squalor should not be ascribed entirely or mainly to
colonial exploitation and neocolonialism either as it is popular to do at
international north-south forums. This is, however, not to deny that
these forces do operate, but when we trace the causes of African underdevelopment to their taproots, we find there as Adam Curle has done
and so poignantly pointed out: "There are problems of separation, dis-
unity and inequality, shown not only in the world and in the national
communities but even at the level of the village."[35] Indeed, as Guy
Hunter warned in the early 1960s: "The economic structure will stand
or fall by reference to the political wisdom and social stability of the
new societies now being born."[36]

Ali Mazrui has reduced the main political problem facing African
countries to two fundamental issues: the crisis of national integration
and the crisis of political legitimacy. Acording to Mazrui, the crisis of
national integration arises when different groups, be they religious as in
Northern Ireland or ethnic as in many parts of Africa, do not yet accept
each other as fellow citizens. The crisis of political legitimacy occurs because significant numbers or groups of citizens do not accept that the
government of the day has the right to rule them—and one may add, in
the manner it is ruling them.[37]

The process of creating a nation out of different ethnic, linguistic, religious, and cultural entities is as complicated as putting together a jigsaw puzzle with many pieces, or manipulating a Chinese tangram to make a new shape. John Dewey used the term "human engineering" to refer to social change effected in a manner tempered with humaneness as the criteria for success. Ali Mazrui has coined the term "cultural engineering"[38] to describe the role of culture as a catalyst in the process of nation-building. The making of new nations has so much in common with the process of constructing a new building that the term nation-building has been most appropriately used. As concrete, columns, and beams are essential to keep a building up and strong, so it is with nations. Pillars have to be erected out of the strengths of the different cultures and beams built across them to keep the new nation together and strong. John Stuart Mill saw a nation as a "portion of mankind . . . united among themselves by common sympathies, which do not exist between them and any other—which make them cooperate with each other more willingly than with other people, desire to be under the same government, and desire that it should be a government by themselves or a portion of themselves exclusively."[39] Rupert Emerson described a nation as "a single people traditionally fixed on a well-defined territory, speaking the same language and preferably a language of its own, possessing a distinctive culture, and shaped to a common mold by many generations of historical experience."[40]

It is clear from the above criteria and the history of the last twenty years that few if any African countries meet the test of nationhood as conceived in nineteenth century Europe, where the aim was to fit people who shared the same culture and language into national states. If anything one should conclude that within the territorial boundaries of each African country there are many nations. What Adam Curle said of Nigeria is true of most countries on the continent: "When Britain granted independence to Nigeria, it was as though Germany or France had been grouped together with, say, Belgium and the Netherlands as a separate nation."[41]

The type of nation-building most appropriate to Africa in terms of present-day realities, however, is not that of a homogenized, monolithic, and monolingual polity analogous to the aims of nineteenth century European nationalism. As J. F. A. Ajayi has stated it: "The fundamental yearning of African nationalism has [always] been to weld peoples speaking different languages and having different traditional cultures into one nation state."[42] In other words, the idea of a melting pot is even more unrealistic in African states than it is in America today. The goal of nation-building in Africa is uniting the different ethnic and cultural entities which existed before the modern states were invented. But regardless of what type of nationalism is envisaged by the founding fathers of African states, a sense of national identity and cohesion in all citizens is definitely essential for economic and social development.

Not much national development can take place in Africa without building a sense of national unity; no great civilizations have ever been built and maintained without hard work animated by and directed to a shared national purpose. The creation of a sense of national unity in Africa, therefore, is one of the most crucial issues during the rest of the twentieth century.

THE ROLE OF THE AFRICAN UNIVERSITY IN NATIONAL INTEGRATION

The universities in Africa should play a leading role in contributing to the solution of national development problems. Among the many questions which should concern African countries today are the following:

How can Africa's vast natural resources best be exploited and utilized by Africans themselves?

How can notions of representative democracy, the sanctity of human life, the supremacy of law, the primacy of the countries' constitutions, and fundamental human rights best be nurtured and maintained?

What are the basic needs of a people who mostly live in rural areas? How can the education systems at all levels best prepare the people of all ages for effectively participating in planning and implementing their own development schemes?

Above all, and most importantly, what is the best means of inspiring a love of country and of creating a "we-feeling" of national identity and belongingness among peoples of diverse ethnic, religious, and cultural backgrounds brought together only recently by colonial accident and not yet having interacted with one another long enough even to evolve a common language, let alone a shared universe of ideas and values?

While it is certainly not the business of the universities alone to provide answers to all the above and to many other intricate problems of national development, it goes without saying that national universities should actively concern themselves with all the problems in their teaching, research, and community service.

A number of African universities have developed programs addressing themselves to some of the above questions. For example, Tanzania requires its secondary school leavers to serve for two years in Ujamaa projects before entering the university. The University of Dar es Salaam, the University of Lagos, and a number of other African universities have developed integrated interdisciplinary courses of African studies which are required of all students regardless of their major fields of study. The University of Sierra Leone through its University College at Njala offers courses leading to a B.Sc., certificates, and diplomas in rural science, agricultural education and home economics. The University of Science and Technology in Ghana, established in 1961, is a pioneer in stimulating grassroots rural technology by making its expertise available to government, industry, and local farmers. It combines teaching, training, research, consultancy, and community service. It trains both high-level and middle-level manpower, under the university umbrella. As part of its research the University of Science and Technology tries to develop new products for local use in farming and small industries.

Another example of innovations that are developing is in the field of primary and teacher education. The University of Ife is involved in the development of primary school curricula that are intended to improve and expand the use of the mother tongue or community languages and to stress local cultures in the elementary schools. University institutes of education including Makerere, University of Sierra Leone, and Dar es Salaam, among others, are involved in the development of primary and teacher education programs aimed at the integration of basic education with rural development. The Department of Agriculture at Makerere requires its second-year students to reside on the university farm and to render extension services to neighboring farmers. The Medical School has for many years run a model health center in a village near Kampala. The major activities of the center include environmental sanitation, curative services, public health visiting and nursing, health education, collection of vital statistics, and the education of mothers in family planning and child care. This model is being extended to other parts of the country where resources permit.

These and a number of others are still, however, few and isolated examples of universities' involvement in nation-building. There is still a great need for the university to study the needs of society and of the economy and to step down to the lowest strata of the community and see things from the grassroots level, where the masses are found.

THE UNIVERSITY AND OTHER LEVELS
OF THE EDUCATION SYSTEM

In most African countries the university is still the guiding star, a magnet that directs all other levels of the education system. The requirements for admission, the structure and nature of its academic offerings affect not only the lives of university students, but have a far-reaching and pervasive trickle-down or ripple effect on the entire education system. When the university requires only purely academic subjects such as physics, chemistry, mathematics, and English for admission to the most sought-after professions, and when it undervalues practical subjects such as agriculture and technical drawing or ignores cultural subjects such as African languages, African music, dance, and drama (as many universities do), these latter subjects will also be ignored by students and their teachers at the secondary schools. Similarly, the primary schools will only emphasize those subjects like English and mathematics which are heavily weighted in the secondary entrance examinations, and will lay less stress on or even completely ignore hygiene, nutrition, community languages, religious education, rural science, and citizenship education, which are of more direct relevance to the lives of the students and their communities. If the university does not have democratic grassroots participation in its structure, if it does not allow students and staff to *live* and practice democracy, nor stress values of mutual respect and cooperative endeavor, nor train teachers animated by these ideals, it will be difficult for such values to flourish in the other levels of the education system. There is need therefore to re-examine the philosophies and systems of studies of African universities from the standpoint of national integration and nation-building.

NEED FOR A PHILOSOPHY OF HIGHER EDUCATION

Before the African university can play a dynamic and positive role in national integration and nation-building, it must begin by clarifying its own philosophy and purpose as the highest institution of learning in the service of a developing society.

There are two vastly divergent views about the function and purpose of a university. The first and perhaps the most commonly held is the concept of the university based on the disinterested pursuit of knowledge and on the international gold standard of scholarship. According to Derek Bok, president of Harvard, the mission of the universities regardless of social, economic, or political conditions is the discovery and transmission of knowledge. Their institutional goal is not to reform society in specific ways. They have neither the mandate nor the competency to set standards of conduct in society or carry out social functions apart from learning and discovery. This ivory tower or monastic type of university is separate and insulated from the mundane concerns of the larger society. Its teaching and research, for example, need not be focused on the here-and-now social problems, but rather on "those purer speculations . . . studies in which the only doubt can be whether the beauty and grandeur of the subjects explored or the precision and cogency of the methods and means of proof deserve our admiration."[43]

In contrast to the orthodox and monastic view is the other concept of the university as a secular community institution seeking knowledge not for its own sake but also instrumentally for the purpose of finding solutions to social problems. This is the type of university which has been advocated by African leaders. Julius Nyerere says:

> The University has not been established purely for prestige purposes. It has a very definite role to play in development in this area, and to do this effectively it must be in, and of the community it has been established to serve. The University of East Africa has to draw upon experience and ideas from East Africa as well as from the rest of the world. And it must direct its energies particularly toward meeting the needs of East Africa.[44]

Benjamin Elija Mays, former president of Morehouse, the college which produced the heroic Martin Luther King, echoes the same com-

mitment to the philosophy of the acquisition or creation of know\
for social use when he says:

> It will not be sufficient for Morehouse College . . . to produce
> clever graduates, men fluent in speech and able to argue their way
> through, but rather honest men, men who are sensitive to wrongs,
> the sufferings and injustices of society, and who are willing to ac-
> cept responsibility for correcting these ills.[45]

Most African universities were initially patterned on the monastic models of the former metropolitan countries. But even after many years of political independence they did little to cut the cultural and academic umbilical cords between themselves and the metropolitan mother institutions. Little was done to evolve new philosophies, aims, and objectives of higher education peculiar to Africa and its problems. Instead, as Godfrey Brown observed: "The War of the Roses went on, and the Wars of Mali and Songhai came in; flora and fauna flown out from England on ice were replaced in practical examinations by local specimens. All the time, however, the pattern of the degree and its form of study remained essentially that of London."[46]

In other words, African universities have so far paid a great deal of attention to three of the main objectives set at Tananarive, namely to teach and advance knowledge through research, to adhere to world academic standards, and to produce high-level manpower.

One major task facing the African university is that of training or educating the whole man for nation-building, to ensure the unification of Africa and to evolve truly African institutions of higher learning dedicated to Africa and its people, yet promoting a bond to the larger human society.

The application of knowledge to social use, and the acceptance of intercultural diversity aimed at promotion of mutual understanding and respect within and among nations ought to be at the core of the philosophy of higher education in Africa and ought to be a main focus of the system of studies in African universities.

THE UNIVERSITY SYSTEM OF STUDIES

One of the most serious defects of higher education in Anglophone Africa is the lack of sufficient provision for the education and training of the individual to become a well-rounded person who is competent in his field but at the same time has functional versatility in other fields. This is because educational systems from the primary school to university are too narrow and geared mainly to the production of students who pass exams rather than students who can do things and to the production of specialists rather than generalists.

University degree programs are for the most part defined in terms of specific academic blocks of three full years. At Makerere University, for example, a student in the Faculty of Arts can take English, French, and Russian on a 3:2:2 or 3:2:1 degree pattern in which the figures indicate a full year's work in a number of disciplines. This means three subjects in the first year and two subjects in the second year and two or one in the final year. If such a student passed English and French in the first year but failed to satisfy examiners in Russian after a supplementary examination, he would have to repeat the entire first year, including those disciplines in which he did well, instead of proceeding to the second-year subject. However, the students study only three subjects, and are generally confined to a particular faculty. Thus a student who is enrolled in the three subjects mentioned above may leave the university not knowing anything about the concepts of social sciences, law, music, dance and drama, and the major cultures in his country.

Narrow specialists are ill-equipped to cope with today's multidimensional and interrelated problems of development requiring multidisciplinary approaches for their solution. Change, be it economic, social, cultural, or political, implies a clear image of the kind of society expected and knowledge of the present and the past. Economic problems have a sociological, political, and cultural set of ramifications and vice versa. Therefore professionals such as doctors, agriculturalists, engineers, teachers, social workers, and so forth, in order to be effective in their work, need not only to master their disciplines but also to know about the dynamics of social change and to be "sensitized to the present and future demands of their societies, oriented toward the development of these societies and conscious of the urgency attached to the process of change."[47]

In pluralistic societies such as we have in Africa, it is imperative that all students and staff, regardless of their main fields of specialization, should have an opportunity to come to grips with problems of nation-building such as interethnic rivalry, race relations, national integration, political legitimacy, the process of cultural and normative fu-

h. They need to reflect on, muse over, and try to under-
ses people to fear and hate rather than to love and trust
hey need to research how patterns of mutual support and
coo....... peration such as Ujamaa, Nyayo, and others can be fos-
tered without destroying cultural identity or individual initiative; and
how we can direct seemingly competing loyalties to family, village, clan,
religion, race, or ethnic origin to common national and human ends.
In other words, as Dewey concluded, "the way to deal with hyphenism
. . . is to welcome it in the sense of extracting from it its special good,
so that it shall surrender into a common fund of wisdom and experience
what it especially has to contribute"[48]—thus making a hyphen separate
as well as united.

Through interdisciplinary courses of study based on national problems and the study and invigoration of local cultures, the African university can act as a catalyst in the development or evolution of national
norms and shared values to bind the many ethnic and cultural groups
together, and thus contribute to the process of national integration. In
this way the university would meet one of the goals of the Tananarive
conference, namely to encourage elucidation and application of African
culture and heritage.

THE UNIVERSITY AND SOCIETY

Another important aspect in the role of the university in nation-
building is the need to establish closer links between itself and society
at large. Universities have been accused of carrying out research on
esoteric problems of little or no import to national development and of
always speaking in a language which only the professional can understand: "The bulk of their writings and their speeches," complained a
Ugandan politician, is "addressed to their colleagues in ex-metropolitan
capitals—London, Paris, Brussels and at times Washington, D.C., Mos-
cow and other capitals."[49] The problems of academic and social distance
between the African university and society are further illustrated by the
following remarks from the Visitation Committee on Makerere University:

> The new university must totally identify itself with the aims of
> society and must play its full part in meeting these goals. . . . We

are satisfied that the standing or the standards of a university are judged not by the extent to which it can meet the demands of international competition for purely academic pursuits, but by the degree to which its products can contribute to the common endeavour to serve the state and answer national problems.[50]

Okot p'Bitek is another perceptive and incisive critic of the African university's failure to dip where it is and to fish in domestic cultural waters. The insistence on rigid formal qualifications for admission and appointment of teachers, for example, and its total dependence on foreign languages and imported knowledge exclude many experts and potential students who would benefit and contribute significantly to higher education and to cultural invigoration in Africa. Okot p'Bitek makes a penetrating indictment:

> You cannot become a member of *their* parliament unless you can speak English or French. You may be the greatest oral historian, but they will never allow you to be anywhere near their university. The greatest traditional musicians and poets cannot teach in the Department of Music or Literature. . . . The African medicine expert is called a "witch doctor" . . . and his skill dubbed fetish. . . . Renowned storytellers, and the greatest dancers cannot teach drama or dancing in their schools and universities. But these men and women are the best in the world in their own field, and no expert, even those professors at the university or anywhere else on earth are qualified to examine them. . . . Our universities and schools are nests in which black exploiters are hatched and bred, at the expense of taxpayers or maybe heartpayers.[51]

Universities in Africa ought to change the color of their image by trying to reach as many people as possible through their extramural or outreach programs, by public discussions, through the mass media, and by correspondence courses on topics and issues impinging, among other things, on national integration and development. The strength of any nation is in its people. Structural or social changes take place insofar as individuals or groups are able to further those values by which they wish to live daily. In other words, the people will contribute to nation-building only to the extent that their values, attitudes, skills, and motivations are consistent with national goals and aspirations. And their contribution will be valuable only to the extent they are convinced that development is possible and that it is through *them*, by *them*, and for *them* that development can be effected. An important role of the university is to enhance this developmental process by directing adequate attention to formal as well as nonformal education at all levels, thereby helping to lift the aspirations of all the people for self-improvement and to close or narrow the gap between the elites and the masses.

TEACHER EDUCATION

And who else can best nurture in the population values, attitudes, and skills favorable to national integration and development? Essentially and significantly, the teacher can, especially in the developing countries where other influences such as the press, radio, and television are timid in scope because of unavailability and also high illiteracy rates. What a single teacher feels, values, knows, and does daily affects the lives of many children. This process repeated over and over again has a great spiraling effect. One of the most direct and effective channels through which the universities can contribute to nation-building is through the education of teachers, particularly of primary school teachers, who teach at that level which is terminal for the majority of those who receive a formal schooling.

Paradoxically, few African universities concern themselves with research in primary education or with the development of curricula and training of teachers for levels below the secondary school. University departments of education concentrate on the preparation of secondary school teachers, and, more often than not, they do not have specialists in elementary and early childhood education, an area which is left entirely to primary teacher training colleges. Elementary school teachers, including primary teacher educators, constitute by far the largest category of public employees in most African countries to be found in every local community. Elementary schools with six or seven teachers each are scattered in all parts of the continent. The most significant channels for improving education and furthering the development of rural areas and the nation is via (1) education of teachers, including headteachers and educators for primary teachers' colleges, and (2) improvement of curricula designed for primary or elementary schools and production of classroom instructional materials. This should be an important and central concern of university institutes and departments of education. Another important role which universities can play in this connection is the training of teachers and community development specialists for mass education.

NEED FOR CLOSER COOPERATION AMONG AFRICAN UNIVERSITIES

Shortage of high-level manpower is still one of the most crippling constraints on African development. There is no field in which the shortage of human capital is more critical than in the area of research producers. Research capabilities are everywhere still very fragile, and in some countries in embryonic stages. And yet research and the implementation of scientific knowledge are so crucial that planned economic and social development is impossible without it. As A. Diop put it so aptly in 1968, "Development is scientific knowledge which has become part of the culture."[52] Through cooperation in the field of research, African universities would be able to make more efficient use of scarce human resources and to have a greater impact on development.

Self-reliance is a useful concept, but problems of development which are multidimensional and international cannot be tackled effectively by each country working alone in isolation. Tsetse flies, mosquitos, animal, plant, and human diseases ignore international boundaries in their movement across the continent. Repeater and dropout rates are everywhere excessively high; the phenomenon of quitting school and the irrelevance of school curricula are common problems in all African countries. Research needed to tackle these problems and to develop appropriate technology for rural transformation may require expensive equipment as well as highly trained personnel. It cannot, therefore, be successfully carried out on a country-by-country basis alone. There is a clear need to establish regional centers of excellence in certain fields for postgraduate training and to build up what Philip Coombs has called research "communities" among African universities.

Cooperation with and among African universities in the area of teacher education was the raison d'être of the AAA/ATEA Program; and research and training, including the establishment of a clearinghouse for the dissemination of research findings, were important aims of the program. Promotion of research capabilities and training of educational leadership made a promising start through the African Fellowships Program and the research of doctoral candidates at Teachers

College. Unfortunately, there was little feedback of the results of this research in the home countries. The clearinghouse was never established, and some of the joint researches discussed at the annual AAA conferences were not implemented. These included the project researches in in-service education suggested at the meeting at Isle of Thorns, the child growth and development proposal discussed at Mohonk, and training and research in educational administration broached at Nairobi. They, however, remain great challenges on the agenda of ATEA for the future.

There are, however, some promising developments. The International Centre for Educational Evaluation (ICEE) at the University of Ibadan, Nigeria (which offers postgraduate training in educational evaluation to students from all over Africa), the African Curriculum Organization (AOC) (which promotes joint research endeavors and sponsors a postgraduate diploma course in curriculum development at Kenyatta University College), and the journal *Education in Eastern Africa* (published spasmodically by the Eastern Regional Council) are examples of possible and fruitful cooperation which have developed since the establishment of ATEA.

Another field in which there is a crying need for inter-university cooperation is that of curriculum development and the production of teaching materials for higher education. We have stressed the need for universities to contribute to African development and social integration. African universities cannot carry out this important task effectively when they are still everywhere depending almost entirely on foreign textbooks and imported knowledge. Cooperation in curriculum research and writing of textbooks addressing African problems would be one way of reducing dependence on foreign teaching materials. This is a major responsibility from which the Association of African Universities (AAU) should not and cannot abdicate. The Association for Teacher Education in Africa made an excellent start in compiling books of readings for Foundations of Education in Africa, a project which is still in progress, but whose completion is long overdue. A more vigorous attack on this problem in all fields is certainly essential.

CONCLUSION

In conclusion, it is necessary to restate the problem. In the last two decades a great deal of investment has been made in education with a view to promoting economic and social development in Africa. National governments devote very high proportions of their recurrent and development budgets to education. Organs of the United Nations, friendly governments, and philanthropic organizations have also directed large sums of money and technical assistance toward education with the hope of lessening the economic and social development gap between Africa and the rest of the world.

The green revolutions that were expected from education, however, have not yet occurred. On the contrary, the scenario that Africa presents after two decades of independence is still one of acute and worsening poverty and social and political turmoil. Although commendable achievements have been made in expanding education and health services, universal primary education is far from being achieved in most African countries, and out of every one hundred babies born to African mothers fifteen to twenty die before they see their first birthday. Even among adults, untimely death still strikes hard in Africa. Although Africa has vast virgin arable lands and enormous economic potential awaiting fuller development, abject poverty, malnutrition, kwashiorkor, and starvation are endemic and widespread throughout the continent. In other words, despite the heavy investment in education, Africa remains a problem continent and a disaster area in perpetual crisis.

What, then, are the prospects of higher education in this problem continent? Problems can be a source of frustration, demoralization, and despair, or a source of stimulation and a challenge for positive change. As Manone points out: Problems can serve as a "launching pad for corrective action or as a terminal of disgust and disarray."[53] No one who knows and loves Africa and particularly African education, as Karl Bigelow did, can bear to take a gloomy view. The peoples of Africa are determined to "make something of themselves, [and] see in education the key to the attainment of their aspirations."[54] This is a great challenge to the national leaders and the educators in Africa to make nation-building and the welfare of the people the focus of all development policies and the core of the education systems.

But nation-building, like development, is a term which is subject to many interpretations and it means different things to different people. To some people nation-building means an increase in the GNP and such things as the expansion in school enrollment; the building of large hospitals, tourist hotels, tarmac roads and bridges; and the number of Mercedes Benzes and Cadillacs driven on them by the ministers and diplomats, as well as the size of the national army. To others, however, nation-building is not concerned simply with the growth of the economy but also and mainly with the improvement in the quality of life of all citizens including their spiritual values and actions, their peace and unity, material well-being, cultural expression, and full participation in civic and national affairs. As Ralph Waldo Emerson's famous dictum from his essay "Civilization" (1870) puts it: "The true test of civilization is, not the census, nor the size of cities, nor the crops—no, but the kind of man the country turns out." All those who are concerned with the development of educational thought at this time, and particularly in higher education, cannot escape the moral responsibility of asking: What kind of men and women do our countries want to turn out—what sort of societies do we want to create? It is through a constant search for the ideal of man, and by its contribution to the kind of man that each country turns out, that higher education will contribute most to nation-building in Africa. As one of the greatest teachers of our time, Julius Nyerere, says: "To build a nation in the true sense is to build the character of its people, of ourselves, to build an attitude of mind which will enable us to live together with our fellow citizens [and those] of the whole world, in mutual friendliness and cooperation."[55]

A crucial role of higher education, as Vice-Chancellor Biobaku succinctly stated it, "is to foster the development of constructive reasoning, objective analysis of problems, courage for one's convictions and loyalty to the ideals of unity among all people composing a nation and between nations."[56] If higher education in Africa is able to do this, and in particular to produce leaders who are inspired and animated by the same ideas and who put the welfare of the people before theirs, it will have played a vital role in the building not only of a new Africa, but also of a new world. This is not a simple task, although it is by no means impossible. The future of education and nation-building in Africa, which Karl Bigelow viewed with optimism and realism, promises "strong seas, and safe harbor."[57]

NOTES

1. Teachers College, *Perspectives on Education*, Spring 1970, p. 14.
2. S. O. Biobaku, adapted from address by Biobaku to 4th Commonwealth Education Conference, Lagos, 1968 (London, HMSO), p. 147.

3. Victor C. Ferkiss, *Africa's Search for Identity* (New York: George Braziller, 1966), p. 40.
4. Lawrence A. Cremin, *The Genius of American Education* (New York: Vintage Books, 1965), p. 4.
5. Jomo Kenyatta, *Facing Mt. Kenya* (New York: Vintage Books, 1965), p. 96.
6. David G. Scanlon, "The Bush School in Africa, Its Educational Problems and Promises," *Phi Delta Kappan* 41, no. 4 (January 1960): 150.
7. Jomo Kenyatta, quoted in C. J. Manone, ed., *Critical Issues in Teacher Education* (Uganda: Kampala, Makerere University, 1970), p. 5.
8. Vincent Mulago, in Kwesi A. Dickson and Paul Ellingworth, eds., *Biblical Revelation and African Beliefs* (Guildford, England: Lutterworth Press, 1969), pp. 137–158.
9. Kofi Busia, *Purposeful Education in Africa* (The Hague: Mouton and Co., 1964), p. 10.
10. T. M. Yusufu, ed., *Creating the African University* (Ibadan, Nigeria: Oxford University Press, 1973), p. 37.
11. Ferkiss, *Africa's Search for Identity*, p. 40.
12. World Bank, *Accelerated Development in Sub-Saharan Africa* (Washington, D.C.: World Bank, 1981), pp. 9–11.
13. E. Jefferson Murphy, *Creative Philanthropy: Carnegie Corporation and Africa 1953–1973* (New York: Teachers College Press, 1976), p. 62.
14. United Nations, "United Nations Development Decade at Mid-Point: An Appraisal by the Secretary General," cited by Colin Leys, *Fifth Commonwealth Education Conference Report*, Canberra, 1971, Appendix 2, p. 5.
15. F. Harbison and C. A. Myers, *Education, Manpower and Economic Growth* (New York: McGraw-Hill, 1964), pp. v, 2.
16. Conference of African States on the Development of Education in Africa, Addis Ababa, 15–25 May 1961, *Final Report* (Paris: United Nations Economic Commission for Africa and United Nations Educational, Scientific and Cultural Organization, 1961), p. 3.
17. Conference of African States on the Development of Education in Africa, Addis Ababa, 15–25 May 1961, *Outline of a Plan for African Educational Development* (Paris: United Nations Economic Commission for Africa and United Nations Educational, Scientific and Cultural Organization, 1961), p. 18.
18. Conference on the Development of Higher Education in Africa, Tananarive, Malagasy Republic, 3–12 September 1962, *The Development of Higher Education in Africa; Report of the Conference* (Paris: UNESCO, 1963), pp. 48–49.

19. Kwame Nkrumah, quoted in Adam Curle, *The Role Developing Societies* (Accra: Ghana University Press, 1 ᠂
20. D. Court, "The Development Ideal in Higher Educal rience of Kenya and Tanzania," *Higher Education* 9, no.
21. World Bank, *Accelerated Development in Sub-Saharan Afr*᠂
22. Samuel Decalo, *Coups and Army Rule in Africa: Studies* ᠂ *Style* (with subsequent adaptations) (New Haven: Yale Un. Press, 1976), pp. 11–12, 26–27.
23. Eni Njoku, "The Modernization of New Nations," in Algo D. Henderson, *Tomorrow's World* (Ann Arbor: University of Michigan Press, 1968), pp. 121–122.
24. S. O. Biobaku, adapted from address by Biobaku to 4th Commonwealth Education Conference, p. 15.
25. ILO, *Ensuring Equitable Growth—Sierra Leone* (Addis Ababa, Ethiopia: International Labour Office, 1981), p. xi.
26. Okot p'Bitek, *Africa's Cultural Revolution* (Nairobi: East African Publishing House, 1973), pp. 8, 9.
27. Ferkiss, *Africa's Search for Identity*, p. 163.
28. John Dewey, *Reconstruction in Philosophy* (New York: Henry Holt and Co., 1919), p. 115.
29. E. Durkheim, *Education and Sociology*, trans. Sherwood Fox (Glencoe, Ill.: Free Press, 1956), p. 28.
30. *Hamlet*, act 3, sc. 1, lines 58–60.
31. E. B. Castle, *Growing Up in East Africa* (London: Oxford University Press, 1966), p. 104.
32. Paulo Friere, "Cultural Action for Freedom," *Harvard Educational Review*, studies I and II (1970).
33. Julius Nyerere, quoted by Manone, ed., *Critical Issues in Teacher Education*, p. 104.
34. Dag Hammarskjöld Foundation, "Seminar on Alternatives and Innovations in Education" (summary), *Development Dialogue*, no. 1 (1980): 135.
35. Curle, *The Role of Education in Developing Societies*, p. 27.
36. Guy Hunter, *Education for a Developing Region* (London: Allen and Unwin, 1963), p. 271.
37. Ali A. Mazrui, *Cultural Engineering and Nation Building in East Africa* (Evanston, Ill.: Northwestern University Press, 1972), p. x.
38. Nazrui, *Cultural Engineering and Nation Building in East Africa*, p. xi.
39. John Stuart Mill, *International Encyclopaedia of the Social Sciences*, vol. 2 (New York: Macmillan, 1968), p. 7.
40. Rupert Emerson, *From Empire to Nation*, cited by N. Konyeaso

Onuoha, "The Role of Education in Nation-Building," *West African Journal of Education* 19, no. 3 (1975).

41. Adam Curle, *Educational Problems of Developing Societies* (New York: Praeger Publishers, 1973), p. 91.

42. Conference on the Development of Higher Education in Africa, Tananarive, Malagasy Republic, September 3–12, 1962, *The Development of Higher Education in Africa; Report of the Conference*, p. 19.

43. Derek Bok, cited by Charles V. Willie, *The Ivory and Ebony Towers* (Lexington, Mass.: Lexington Books, 1981), p. 107.

44. Julius Nyerere, cited by Karl W. Bigelow, in Manone, ed., *Critical Issues in Teacher Education*, p. 310.

45. Benjamin Mays, cited by Willie, *The Ivory and Ebony Towers*, p. 107.

46. Godfrey N. Brown and M. Hiskett, *Conflict and Harmony in Education in Tropical Africa* (Madison, N.J.: Fairleigh Dickinson University Press, 1975), p. 133.

47. A. Wandira, in Manone, ed., *Critical Issues in Teacher Education*, p. 49.

48. Dewey, *Reconstruction in Philosophy*, p. 115.

49. N. Akena-Adoko, "The Role of the Intellectual in the African Revolution," *East Africa Journal* (March 1969), p. 23.

50. Makerere University Visitation Committee (1970), cited by C. W. de Kiewiet, *The Emergent African University—An Interpretation* (Washington, D.C.: Overseas Liaison Committee, American Council on Education, 1971), p. 54.

51. p'Bitek, *Africa's Cultural Revolution*, p. 58.

52. A. Diop, cited by Michael Bohnet and Hans Reichert, eds., *Applied Research and Its Impact on Economic Development: The East African Case* (New York: Humanities Press, 1972), p. 86.

53. C. J. Manone, *The Improvement of Education in Thailand* (prepared under AID Contract 493–038T, 1973), p. 27.

54. K. W. Bigelow, "Problems and Prospects of Education in Africa," in P. H. Coombs and K. W. Bigelow, *Education and Foreign Aid* (Cambridge, Mass.: Harvard University Press, 1965), pp. 73–74.

55. Julius Nyerere, cited by K. W. Bigelow, in Manone, ed., *Critical Issues in Teacher Education*, pp. 97–98.

56. S. O. Biobaku, adapted from address by Biobaku to 4th Commonwealth Education Conference, p. 157.

57. K. W. Bigelow, "Problems and Prospects of Education in Africa," in Coombs and Bigelow, *Education and Foreign Aid*, p. 74.

Current Trends in Teacher Education in English-Speaking Africa

A. R. THOMPSON

Centre for Overseas Studies
School of Education, University of Bristol

It is a great pleasure for me to return to Ibadan again and meet with so many old friends. It is also an honor, though at the same time a sad duty, to have been invited to give this lecture in memory of Karl Bigelow, a man for whose vision, energy, and dedication I had the highest respect. I was happy to listen to the sincere tributes paid to him by so many distinguished African educators this morning. However, if I may paraphrase Shakespeare, I come not to praise Karl Bigelow but in some small measure to help promote the continuance of his work. If he were here today, and who knows, he may well be here somewhere, he would be saying to himself "Cut the cackle, Thompson, let's get down to business," and that, Mr. Chairman, with your permission, is what I intend to do.

FACTORS LEADING TO CHANGE

In *The World Education Crisis* (1968) Philip Coombs argued that

educational systems will not be modernized until the whole system of teacher training is drastically overhauled, stimulated by peda-

---

Lecture delivered on May 11, 1982, at Ibadan University, Nigeria.

gogical research, made intellectually richer and more challenging, and extended far beyond preservice training into a system for continuous professional renewal and career development for *all* teachers.[1]

Such calls as this have been frequently heard over the last quarter of a century, notably in the conferences of the Association for Teacher Education in Africa (ATEA) and its eastern and western regional councils. Yet it is worth reflecting for a moment upon the circumstances that have arisen since 1968 that have given new point and urgency to this kind of statement and may have at last initiated an era of exciting change in teacher education.

The massive expansion of educational systems, particularly at the primary level with the adoption of universal education policies in a number of countries, has involved in a subtle and not always fully comprehended way a transition from a highly selective structure designed to produce the managerial, technical, and intellectual elites upon whom national development was thought to depend, toward a mass education system, the economic returns from which though arguably significant were less important than the political and social returns in a period when equity, social justice, and political stability were seen to be vitally interlinked.

This rapid expansion has been followed more slowly by curricular and structural reform as consciousness dawned that not merely had traditional schooling not produced the anticipated benefits to society as a whole but that mass education in the absence of economic growth and development to absorb the products of the school might well prove a wasteful and possibly dysfunctional investment. Social justice might well demand equality of opportunity to compete for the glittering prizes of the modern sector and the school system might still have to provide the ladder of upward social mobility to meet the high level manpower requirements of the nation, but at the same time far more effective provision had to be made for the needs of the growing numbers of pupils unlikely to find a place on that ladder.

Consequently, in many African countries we have been seeing the painful and inevitably slow process of redirecting the curriculum toward studies more closely related to the local community and the world of work. At the same time, the 1970s have seen a vigorous movement in the direction of mass education from another direction, that of non-formal education, for which its advocates have claimed greater flexibility, more immediate payoff, and potentially greater cost-effectiveness than traditional schooling. Schools have themselves been called upon to link more effectively with local grassroots communities, to serve the total learning needs of such communities, and to integrate more closely with nonformal provision in nationwide learning systems, diverse enough to be responsive to the needs of many different groups without "shunting any group . . . into dead-end educational channels or inferior learning options."[2]

In my recent book, *Education and Development in Africa*,[3] I have sought to analyze more fully the nature of these shifts in educational thinking. In any case there is little need in such a gathering as this to develop this theme further. The essential point I am making is that such educational reform is clearly dependent for its success largely upon the caliber of the staff responsible for putting it into effect. Yet the re-direction of educational processes, and curricular and structural reform means not only that new kinds of instructors or educators are needed, as in adult education or community-oriented studies, but that serving teachers find that to a considerable extent their knowledge and skills, their initial training, and their store of experience have become inadequate and to some extent at least irrelevant. It may be argued that for these reasons the current concept of the qualified teacher has become obsolete in many situations. Consequently, the need for updating and refresher courses for serving teachers has become increasingly urgent.

Allied to this is the fact that in many countries the expansion of school systems has made available to the teaching profession larger numbers of entrants with at least some secondary education; training programs recruiting from these levels have been redesigned and the basic level of certification raised. Each change in the curriculum of initial teacher education and each raising of the minimum level of certification leave large numbers of serving teachers in possession of obsolete and inadequate qualifications. At the same time in some countries a counter-vailing tendency has been noted. Expansion, it is claimed, has led to lower standards of performance in schooling so that the quality of teacher education, dependent upon the underlying quality of the personal education received by its entrants, has been undermined. In consequence of such trends, the demand has risen for far greater upgrading opportunities both from serving teachers seeking more secure status and improved career opportunities and from systems managers wishing to phase out obsolete grades of teaching staff.

Whatever its effects upon trained teacher quality, there is no doubt that one of the most crucial factors leading to the current reappraisal of teacher education has been the extent to which expansion of education has involved the employment of large numbers of untrained teachers in many countries. A recent survey showed that the proportion of un-qualified primary teachers ranges from 71 percent in Liberia and 68 per-cent in The Gambia, to around 20 percent in Malawi, Zambia, and Uganda. In Nigeria, it is reported, this proportion ranges from 94 per-cent in Niger and Borno states to over 50 percent even in some tradi-tionally more advantaged southern states.

The urgent need to find new and substantially cheaper ways of training new teachers and the large backlog of unqualified serving teach-ers has achieved what years of academic discussion failed to achieve—active policies of review and reform of initial teacher education programs and strategies. While at the present time attention inevitably focuses upon the primary level of schooling, it is apparent that in a number of countries further education and training may have to be provided for the products of universal primary education in response to inevitable strong social pressure.

Meanwhile the growing size and complexity of education systems and the need to adapt them to new situations have created a need for a greater degree of specialization among education staff. The teaching pro-fession can no longer be regarded as a profession of teachers and training for membership can no longer be regarded as simply concerned with classroom operations. As Newman Smart forecast a few years ago, "The job of teaching will grow in sophistication and into specialised functions. The simple teacher will continue to be transformed into the curriculum expert, the adult educator, the extension worker, the educational admin-istrator and planner, the school counsellor, and so on."[4]

New roles and responsibilities are being created within schools; outside them, duties such as supervision and inspection, materials pro-duction and distribution, the conduct of examinations, and teacher edu-cation itself, often in the past largely undertaken by general education staff, are now seen as requiring specially trained staff if reasonable levels of efficiency are to be maintained. Once again logistic and technical considerations are making a necessity of courses of action teacher educators have long urged as being desirable in principle, and provision for the retraining of staff for new roles is now beginning to receive a higher degree of priority.

Finally I am optimistic enough to believe that two other factors are beginning to have a serious impact upon the way in which we look at teacher education. The first arises from the enormous difficulty being experienced in making effective the kinds of qualitative change discussed above and so attractive in theory. Experience in many parts of the world appears to suggest that educational systems are very difficult to change fundamentally, that while superficial structural and indeed curricular change can be achieved, real change in the functions of schooling and the nature of what actually happens in the classroom is enormously difficult for reasons that relate to the many inertial factors that lie at the heart of the systems themselves and their societal context. Of the former, perhaps the main reason is the labor intensive nature of the education industry, its dependence not upon plant and equipment so much as upon personnel. To change education may mean changing the personnel who are serving in the system, personnel who, for reasons of training, morale, and motivation, may be inclined to prefer the security of that which is familiar and accustomed to the risks and added work loads of innovation. Studies of the management of innovation suggest that we have seriously overestimated the capacity of power coercive, center-periphery, top-down processes to bring about change without the willing, positive, and informed cooperation of those whose working procedures are being changed. Consequently, much attention has been focused upon rational-empirical and normative re-educative processes of innovation,[5] processes that are not necessarily mutually exclusive but that may be called into play even within essentially centralized systems such as most African countries have and may have to retain as long as education is primarily regarded as an investment in planned national development. Consequently we need to review training procedures and ask to what extent they can create the kind of professional responsiveness and initiative in teachers that appear necessary to support educational reform.

Such measures are particularly important in those countries where the expansion of educational systems has presented problems of financing, administering, and supervising local schools, and where it is recognized that relevance to local community needs cannot easily be achieved by common programs designed at a distance. Several countries have therefore, as a matter both of expediency and policy, begun to move in the direction of decentralization and indeed devolution of responsibility for decision-making. The success of such policies will depend upon the caliber of educational personnel serving in the field and upon a quite radical transformation in the nature of their training and in the training of those who will retain overall supervisory coordinating responsibilities.

The second factor influencing the way we look at teacher education is that many of the kinds of change that our policymakers envisage are in directions with which we have relatively little experience or our experience has been little analyzed and understood. Consequently, we cannot claim to possess genuine expertise in such fields as community schooling, prevocational studies, production activities, and links with nonformal education that would permit us easily to design the innovation and immediately train the staff who are to carry it into effect. Instead we must recognize that we are feeling our way toward new approaches, that our staff must be competent enough and motivated enough to develop their own experience through initiating, implementing, and evaluating activities related to the agreed theme.

Again we are beginning to ask to what extent conventional patterns and programs of teacher education are capable of producing educationists able to develop their academic and professional knowledge and skills and to draw upon their own experience and that of others to undertake this development role more effectively. To many of us this concept of professionality among educationists is fundamental to our views of educational advancement, yet many of the procedures we have up to now employed to equip our staff appear better calculated to increase their dependence upon close direction and supervision than to promote their capacity for independent operation.

Of course, there is an alternative view that argues that our teaching forces are so ill qualified and poorly motivated that they cannot be considered as being within reach of the threshold of professionality that they must be ready to cross before we can implement innovation strategies of the kind we are here discussing. I can do no better than to quote from the report of the UNESCO Asian regional seminar held at Chiangmai, Thailand, in October, 1978, and to suggest that we need urgently to consider whether we agree, for upon our decision depends our whole view of the nature of teacher education:

The teacher "can perhaps no longer consider himself strictly or only as a 'professional' who is completely free to experiment and do his own research. He may have to settle, more commonly, for being a civil servant in the full sense, perhaps a technician, a para-professional, a manager of the learning process . . . an agent of change rather than an initiator of change."[6]

I would hope that we would reject this view and seek ways whereby we may slowly but steadily increase the professionality of our teachers, accepting that though the road may be long it will lead us in the direction we want to go, toward lively and vigorous schools constantly seeking qualitative improvement and responding promptly to social change.

If we wish our teachers to be technicians, perhaps the reforms we may need to make in teacher education are minimal. If we want to create a committed body of professionals, the change needed may be considerable. Before examining teacher education as it is practiced at present, I think, however, it is necessary to make a vitally important general point that is too often overlooked. The creation of an effective teaching force for the years ahead certainly depends in part upon training—and I do not find it offensive to use the word training in connection with professional development—but it also depends upon other things as well. We need to see training in a wider context, which I would refer to as staff development and utilization.

The professional teacher needs knowledge and he needs skills, but he also needs to be appropriately motivated; otherwise he may not make use of his knowledge and skills. Furthermore, he needs genuine opportunity to apply and sharpen his skills, by which I mean not merely the materials and working conditions to make it possible for him to function effectively, though these are certainly local conditions and needs as he sees them, and so he strays from the narrow track that official policy may appear to dictate.

Thus the process of staff development and utilization to which I refer will include

Improved selectivity and methods of selection of entrants to the profession insofar as circumstances allow.

Training to equip entrants with the knowledge and skills they will require, including the skills of independent judgment and self-evaluation.

Deployment and induction to ensure that staff are located accord-

ing to their qualifications and experience for maximum effectiveness and given the opportunity and assistance to grow into their
new posts, both initially and at later stages in their careers.
Motivation to encourage them to perform to the best of their
ability, which may involve a range of measures. These may include the development of more attractive and functional career
structures, patterns of reward and recognition, more dynamic
structures of professional association to break down the isolation
in which teachers commonly operate, and clear areas of professional responsibility within which they may apply their own
judgment.
Re-training at appropriate points in their careers, whether to update
or upgrade them or to equip them for new roles and positions.
Provision of support services in the form of supportive and advisory
rather than purely inspectorial supervision, and access to resources, materials, and information.

In creating the kind of profession that will sustain qualitative improvement, all these elements are likely to be important, and, though
the utopia in which all will be available is a long way off, we need perhaps to ask ourselves to which of these elements priority needs to be
given at particular stages in our progress. In some circumstances this
training provision upon which we lavish so much attention may be less
significant than some of the other measures to which I have drawn
attention.

RESISTANCE TO CHANGE

Let us return to the subject of teacher education and training itself.
Having myself argued for some time the need to understand the strong
inertial forces at work in education systems, I was intrigued to note that
Torsten Husen believes: "The teacher training system appears to be the
most rigid and conservative part of a national educational system."[7] Is
this so? If it is, there are a number of reasons that might be advanced to
account for it.

Because of the low academic standards of many entrants into initial
training, and because teacher educators and others have always asserted
the primacy of teachers knowing the subject matter of what they teach,

college programs have often been heavily burdened with academic content. The status of these subjects vis-à-vis professional studies has been enhanced by two factors. The first, significant in its own right, has been the low standard of motivation to enter the profession of many entrants who see teacher education as a second or third choice substitute for secondary or higher education and wish to retain a wider range of career options than a narrow teaching focused program might itself afford. The second is that professional studies are largely different from academic studies in that they involve relatively less content to be learned and a higher degree of sustained reflection and thought, the value of which is not readily apparent to students raised in classrooms where content learning for examination purposes has been the norm.

The outcome has often been a hierarchy of esteem with academic subjects receiving the largest proportion of student attention and effort, with academic discipline studies in psychology and sociology, in particular, ranking second, leaving classroom-oriented practical and methodological studies at the bottom of the heap. Such status considerations both restrict the possibilities of restructuring and reform and reduce the effect of changes in the direction of more effective school focused training. One outcome has tended to be that curricular changes in teacher education have largely involved accretion rather than more fundamental structural reform. The search for qualitative improvement in teacher education has taken the form of lengthening courses of training, increasing the capacity of colleges in terms of student numbers, and impeding consideration of the reallocation of funds within teacher education systems. The finance available has commonly permitted little more than an expansion of the existing patterns.

The staffing of teacher education has also presented structural rigidities. At a time when educational expansion inevitably involved spreading highly qualified, experienced, and competent staff more thinly, teacher education has commonly received perhaps surprisingly low priority. As John Turner has suggested, "in many countries Teacher Training is considered a low status activity, conducted in low status institutions."[8] Many colleges continue to be staffed inadequately, and largely with staff who themselves may possess academic qualifications but little experience in the classrooms. For teachers themselves, teacher education has often appeared to be a cul-de-sac in career terms. The traditional route to achievement has been through the schools, particularly in the move from primary to secondary teaching and from teaching to administrative and supervisory posts. Rarely is teacher education seen as an attractive career step. In some systems staff have been transferred freely between secondary and teacher training institutions with the consequence that it has proved difficult to build up a cadre of committed and experienced teacher educators.

Under such circumstances innovation has not been favored. Indeed insofar as new demands have been placed on the schools, such as community leadership and prevocational work, or production related activities, teacher education staff lacking real competence in these areas have experienced growing insecurity. This has reinforced their inclination to cling to accustomed teaching methods and content. The demands of expansion on the colleges that have commonly resulted in overcrowded classes and pressures upon library and other resources have tended to cause increased reliance upon lecture methods, and have, somewhat paradoxically, reinforced the prevailing concentration upon in-house residential programs at the expense of patterns of outreach into the schools. Husen himself appears to believe that an important reason for the conservatism of teacher education is the inclination of those serving in the colleges to assert their own interests through lengthening training periods and expanding their empires.[9]

The problems of the initial training institutions have been compounded by their relative isolation not merely from each other and from the mainstream of educational rethinking—the latter often reflected in the deplorable standard of colleges libraries for staff and students—but from other branches of the education service with which their function in theory is closely linked. Colleges rarely have the capacity to follow up their students once they have been allocated to schools. Commonly this task is assumed to be performed by the inspectorates, but rarely is there direct feedback by the inspector to the colleges, or adequate common understanding of the qualities required by the serving teacher. Curriculum development centers and materials production units are not well known for their success in synchronizing the introduction of new syllabuses and materials into schools with changes in the training of teachers to use them. The inclination of such centers has been to rely on inservice courses for serving teachers and to understress the necessary adjustment in initial training, particularly serious in expanding educational systems where so much reliance must be placed upon recently trained teachers.

Let me recall what I have been saying. It has been suggested that teacher education has on the whole been highly conservative, and that if this is so there appear to be many good reasons why it is so. The picture drawn in the foregoing is a gloomy one, but is it in fact a true picture? The answer for this writer is that it is not entirely true. Certainly I would agree that a high proportion of teacher education is conducted on traditional lines, has shown little sign of revitalizing itself, and is of unsatisfactory quality. But now we must look at the rest of the picture and we will see it is one that reveals a surprising vitality and a range of so far largely experimental and unevaluated developments that merit our study.

Before doing so, however, let me repeat my earlier assertion that, sadly perhaps, such changes as we are about to examine in teacher education systems stem not from the thinking and research of many committed teacher educators over the last two decades so much as from the exigencies of scale and costs. In consequence, we cannot assume too readily that innovations that have taken place are likely to remain permanent features of our teacher education systems and we shall note instances where revision to traditional practice is already taking place.

INITIAL TRAINING PROGRAMS

Here the main factor by far has been the need to equip greatly expanded school systems with adequately competent teachers at minimum cost. The high unit cost of conventional residential training programs and the logistics of expansion, even given the financial resources, have led a number of African countries to seek cheaper and larger scale ways of training teachers, commonly utilizing sandwich or correspondence cum contact techniques.

When in 1974 Tanzania decided to move toward universal primary education, it found that it needed almost to double its primary teacher force. The cost of doing so by means of college training would have involved an annual cost substantially in excess of the total recurrent annual budget for education as a whole. Sheer necessity therefore forced Tanzania to adopt a distance training approach whereby student teachers are appointed to schools to teach a maximum of fifteen periods per week in standards 3 or 4 under close supervision by class or subject teachers. They follow courses provided by radio and correspondence provided by the Institute of Education and Institute of Adult Education and supported by previously trained division or ward education officers, each of whom provides face-to-face contact with around ten to fifteen students in his charge. Each student receives a stipend but the total cost per student teacher is nevertheless only three thousand shillings per annum instead of fifteen thousand shillings in a college, and the student teachers are able to contribute immediately to the teaching program of the schools where they are located. The target figure has now been reached and the program has been substantially reduced in scale. Tanzania has retained its conventional colleges and increased their number, but has reduced the length of the residential program from three to two years for Grade C teachers and from two to one year for better qualified Grade A teachers. As yet neither the distance program nor the reduced residential programs have been fully evaluated, though some reduction in quality has been anticipated. It may be that lessons will have been learned from both measures and that actions taken as a response to an emergency situation may justify their retention as permanent features of the system.

A similar situation faced Nigeria, though on a far greater scale, necessitating a more highly institutionalized response. The introduction of universal primary education demanded the production of 290,000 new teachers by 1982, a figure well beyond the capacity of conventional colleges in spite of the creation of over sixty new colleges. The long established Teacher In-Service Education Project (TISEP), directed by Ahmadu Bello University Institute of Education with local coordination provided by state ministries of education, had through correspondence cum contact methods developed a capacity to train four thousand teachers at a time for the nine northern states, but the overwhelming scale of the need appeared to necessitate a far larger and national program. In 1976 the National Teachers' Institute (NTI) at Kaduna was set up to employ correspondence cum contact techniques involving the use of carefully prepared self-instructional modules and the creation of one field center and several study centers in each of the nineteen states. When fully operational, the NTI aims to provide training for unqualified and subqualified serving teachers numbered in hundreds of thousands, and eventually will develop upgrading programs for several categories of qualified teachers, awarding its own certificate, diplomas, and even degrees. Such a project has involved massive investment and NTI offers every prospect of being a permanent and even dominant feature of teacher education in Nigeria.

On attaining independence, Zimbabwe gave high priority to its integrated teacher education course (ZINTEC), introduced in 1981. The program is designed to train and certificate untrained serving teachers through a four-year course comprising an initial residential course of sixteen weeks in one of four new regional colleges, correspondence cum contact courses provided from five new regional centers while the teachers continue to teach in the schools, and a final sixteen-week residential course in the colleges. Since the trainees will possess at least five O-level passes, the training is entirely professional and each regional center will have a capacity to handle 750 teachers. It is estimated that the program will produce the required number of trained teachers at one-third the cost of conventional college-based programs. These will nevertheless continue to operate in parallel to ZINTEC. Again, and perhaps surprisingly, it appears to be assumed that ZINTEC will be phased out once the target figure is reached.

William Pitcher College in Swaziland has since 1978 focused its in-service activities upon the training of unqualified serving teachers. Following criticism of the academic quality of entrants, it revised the program to provide a two-year training period during which trainees will spend one term each year in college and follow correspondence cum contact programs while serving in school. When the project ends this year [1982], about half the primary teachers in Swaziland will have been trained by these means. Advocates point to the effectiveness and low cost of the program. Nevertheless, it appears to have been decided to revert to conventional teacher training in spite of the intended move toward universal primary education in 1985.

The National Teacher Training College (NTTC) in Lesotho, established in 1975, has adopted an interesting sandwich pattern for its four current programs of initial training. Each program lasts three years with the second year being an internship during which students are placed at one of thirty-four internship schools to work under a full-time experienced tutor with regular support from the NTTC tutors. However, to this set of programs was added in 1976 the Lesotho In-Service Education for Teachers (LIET) program, which has in principle the capacity to offer upgrading opportunities to primary or secondary teachers at no fewer than seven levels. Priority is, however, being given in the meantime to unqualified primary school teachers who receive periodic on-campus courses totaling ten weeks, together with two years of correspondence courses while serving in their schools. Academic courses are provided by the Lesotho Distance Teaching Centre, and professional courses by the NTTC, which offers the support of field staff. Currently, thirty-five Educational Resource Centres are being set up at the field centers to support both the NTTC and the LIET programs.

Until such programs as these have been properly evaluated, it would be premature to argue too strongly for their permanent retention. But school-based training may be seen not simply as a means of alleviating the effects of teacher shortage by keeping trainees in post, but as a means of establishing a closer functional link between colleges and schools whereby new ideas and methods may be steadily and regularly infused into the latter and whereby the training received may be more relevant and practical and more effectively absorbed through the opportunities available for its immediate application. It would be unwise to overlook the very real difficulties of providing genuinely suitable correspondence materials and of maintaining face-to-face contact between tutors and trainees—programs similar to those mentioned above have been impossible to maintain at Buloba, Masindi, and Kabwangasi colleges in Uganda for obvious reasons—but there is a clear case for careful consideration to be given to the lessons of experience in such programs as I have described.

OTHER TRAINING PROGRAMS

The widely faced crisis in unqualified serving teachers has inevitably meant that much lesser priority has been allocated to upgrading, retraining, and refresher programs. Perhaps only in Nigeria has upgrading been made available to teachers on a substantial scale. Here the universities have responded to the need by developing a range of part-time sandwich and correspondence courses leading to recognized intermediate level qualifications as well as offering the conventional range of higher degree programs that are, of course, only open to the already well qualified. When the National Teachers' Institute is fully operative and B.Ed. programs are widely developed as is intended by universities and advanced teachers' colleges, Nigeria will possess unrivaled upgrading capacity.

Malawi and Kenya have, however, valuable experience in upgrading programs provided by means of broadcasting, a medium that has perhaps surprisingly not been widely used for teacher training purposes in most African countries.

The Malawi Correspondence College and Broadcasting Unit established in 1965 has, since 1968, provided upgrading courses for qualified teachers in association with Domasi In-Service Centre through a combination of correspondence, a series of thirty weekly radio programs, and short residential courses. The Kenya Correspondence Course Unit was set up in 1967 to provide two years of secondary education to poorly qualified primary school teachers. The course, known as the distance program, is based on carefully structured guides together with more conventional study materials, weekly radio broadcasts, submission of assignments, and face-to-face contact with tutors during vacations. It leads to the Junior Secondary Examination and will, it is hoped, lead to the phasing out of the P3 grade of teacher. The experience of these programs should be of wide interest.

In Kenya between 1968 and 1972 the pass rate for the distance program was significantly higher than that of students enrolled in schools and the cost was significantly lower. However, in the later years as the number of students enrolled declined, the high fixed costs of the program meant that unit costs rose significantly. More generally it has been suggested that distance programs of this kind may be more suited to the raising of academic qualifications of teachers, that the payoff in terms of improved classroom teaching is uncertain, and that for professional improvement regular tutorial support together with residential periods are indispensable.

There also has been a significant, if modest, development of provision for the training of specialist cadres of education staff. Ministry and in a few cases university-linked programs for the training of headmasters, ranging from one year to a few days, are reported from Zambia, Botswana, Ghana, Liberia, Uganda, Zimbabwe, and Nigeria; for training teachers' college tutors from notably Lesotho, Zambia, Zambabwe, Botswana, and Kenya. There is also growing interest in inspectorate training in a number of countries and much has already been achieved in Nigeria in this respect. An interesting program in Plateau State of Nigeria seeks to train senior teachers to supervise and assist unqualified teachers in their own schools. A similar development is reported from Tanzania. There is a growing awareness that mass education systems are being adversely affected by poor administration; particular attention is now being given to the proper training of administrators at all levels of the system. To a considerable extent, however, retraining remains dependent upon access to overseas courses though there are indications of institutional developments that will reduce this dependence.

In most African countries a wide range of short courses has for many years been provided by a wide range of agencies to prepare teachers for curriculum change or for general refresher purposes. Few recent developments are reported in this respect and there remains little empirical evidence to suggest that courses of this kind have any significant effect upon teaching and learning in the classroom. The participation of teachers' unions and associations in the provision of such courses as in The Gambia and Ghana is a potentially valuable development where we are concerned with generating genuine professional responsibility among our teachers. There is also much of interest in the training potential of the range of support services for teachers now being developed in some countries.

In many African countries there is growing recognition of the need to provide even fully qualified teachers with continuing support. In part this stems from concern that new training structures may take time to become effective and that the scale and experimental nature of some programs may involve some reduction in quality. While this is not a necessary consequence of new approaches, it is not uncommon or unexpected for reservations to be expressed about the quality of teachers trained by unconventional means. More significantly, however, and irrespective of the form of initial training provided, it is understood that the effects of training are likely to be limited, particularly in circumstances of professional isolation. Support services that reinforce training and facilitate application of what is learned during training, and that in themselves contribute to ongoing professional development are increasingly seen as a vital part of the staff development continuum. Again, however, while many African countries are setting about the task, a number of very different policies is being pursued.

The move toward more advisory and less inspectorial patterns of supervision, such as has been widely advocated in principle, has perhaps not gone very far, partly because of the desire of education authorities to retain control over expanding systems largely staffed by unqualified teachers, but also because of the inevitable conflict between the advisory role and the inspectorial role. Although provision of training for inspectors has been stepped up in recent years as in many Nigerian states, rarely have inspectorates been sufficiently well staffed to permit the kind of regular contact with the schools required by an advisory service. We have seen, in consequence, the emergence of new catgories of support staff variously termed mobile teacher trainers as employed in the primary education improvement project in northern Nigeria, supervisory headmasters as also used in some northern Nigerian states, itinerant teacher educators in Tanzania, and subject organizers in Ghana.

Such measures that take training to the schools instead of bringing teachers to the often artificial and remote environment of a training center may not merely prove cheaper but more effective in that they may increase the degree of teacher involvement in training and encourage techniques that will promote the growth of self-confidence and initiative upon which genuine professional growth may largely be based. They open the door further for the fuller development of school-based programs in which the whole staff of a school may participate in such a way as to deal with the specific problems of their school. This is potentially more effective than releasing one staff member to attend a course in the often vain hope that he will then have the status and leadership capacity to convert his colleagues. Similarly, the door is being opened to school-focused activities in which staff from a group of schools may come together to study their common problems cooperatively in a process of self-training.

New institutional frameworks for teacher support services have been developed in several African countries. Resource centers and teachers' centers of different kinds have been developed in Kenya, Nigeria, Zambia, Botswana, Lesotho, and Sierra Leone, but as yet few firm conclusions can be reached about their effect. Where strong and well-staffed centers have been created, they often suffer from geographical remoteness from teachers and schools and tend to become in-service training centers to which teachers are drawn for occasional courses. They may also suffer from being managed independently of other teacher training institutions. Those centers that have been provided as integral parts of specific programs possess a clear focus that may contribute to their success.

There may be particular interest in the efforts being made in a number of countries to develop a new kind of teachers' college. In these countries, H. W. Hawes reports, there is beginning a change of emphasis "which sees a college far more as an education centre of an area for school teachers and adult teachers, for pre-service and in-service, for local curriculum development, and as a resource centre for aids and materials rather than just as a place primarily where young men and women are turned into teachers."[10] At Bunumbu in Sierra Leone, for instance, the intention is to produce a new kind of teacher for the rural areas whose involvement with the community will not be limited to teaching its children. But it has been recognized that reforming the curriculum of training is likely to be inadequate without direct support to the schools and communities in which the teachers will serve. Consequently the project, which began in 1973, has sought to make the college a focal point for schools within a twenty-mile radius that are to be developed as community centers, and consideration is now being given to its replication. Clearly the concept is easier to formulate than to implement and there will be much interest in the findings of the evaluation study that has been undertaken.

However, a somewhat different trend may be identified in Botswana. When that country established its mobile in-service team in 1973, members of the team were based at the three teacher training colleges and were expected to spend one-third of their time teaching initial training courses and the remainder in advising schools and conducting workshops largely for the production by teachers of low cost teaching material. In this way initial and in-service training were to be linked and the college accepted some responsibility for the latter. Two years later, however, the team was reconstituted in the rural areas with each member of the team working more closely with the schools. From 1978 a new link with the colleges was created with the establishment of purposely built specialist teachers' centers on the college campuses, but later other centers were set up independently of the colleges and no very effective symbiosis between centers and colleges was achieved. More recently, in-service training has been amalgamated with school inspection. This may further separate pre-service from in-service training.

In other countries a further trend may be identified: the establishment of national centers for the conduct of in-service training. Whereas in Malawi the transformation of the Domasi In-Service into the Malawi Institute of Education is accompanied by a substantial devolution of in-service training to the national teacher training colleges, elsewhere the task is increasingly being allocated to specialist centers such as the National In-Service Training College (NISTCOL) at Chalimbana in Zambia, the National Teachers' Institute at Kaduna in Nigeria, the Education Staff Institute at Kenyatta University College in Kenya (KESI), and the LIET unit at the National Teacher Training College in Lesotho mentioned above. Ghana is also considering a similar move. The arguments for this development are also persuasive. For in-service training effectively coupled with outreach to schools, a substantial core staff of trained specialists may be necessary. This staff can only be maintained in a permanent institution. There they will be protected against being diverted into other tasks seen as being more central, as is all too likely to happen in a multipurpose institution. Moreover, the training of senior staff and the infusion of new dynamic concepts of administration and educational development into the higher reaches of the system may perhaps be best achieved through institutions of high status and influence. Through such institutions, operating close to decision-making circles, communication and improved understanding between policymakers and implementers may perhaps be achieved. Finally, such institutions may have a research and evaluative capacity, the results of which may be diffused into the system through the training programs.

There are, however, some dangers in employing centralized and powerful institutions of this kind, notably in that training may be removed from the field and become formalized, theoretical, and prescriptive. Consequently it may become more suited to the improvement of conventional and existing procedures than to the promotion of participative and more professional modes of working, which may be more appropriate in those countries seeking more decentralized patterns of administration and re-schooling. There is a further question to which I shall return about the relationship of such centers to universities. In more general terms, one may have reservations about what may be a growing compartmentalization of professional training whereby initial and in-service training, which should be planned as a continuum, may be fixed as highly distinct operations because they are conducted by different institutions. Teacher educators should watch these trends with considerable interest.

The kinds of development I have described and others that I have not are to many of us exciting and hopeful. Though conceived in response to practical exigencies of scale and costs, they should be examined carefully for the potential they offer in terms of genuine qualitative improvement. Some word of caution is necessary. The trends and developments described are still limited in scale across Africa and are often in the very early stages of development. There is a great gulf, as we all know, between intentions and effective implementation. It should recall Nyerere's words of warning to ardent friends of Tanzania: "If we state that some new Jerusalem is where we are going, and then we begin the journey, our friends should not be disappointed when they find that we are still in the desert."[11]

Across the continent the conventional remains the convention; the initial training college still reigns relatively supreme; and in-service programs, where the greater number of innovations currently exists, still tend to be regarded as second-best, temporary expedients, a cluster of firefighting techniques, eventually no longer to be needed, for remedying temporary weaknesses in the initial training provision. Experiments are being initiated by a wide range of agencies. Sadly in my view, a leading role continues to be played by external funding bodies. The structure whereby teacher education may be coordinated, planned, and evaluated is even nonexistent in many countries. Many of the more innovative developments have taken place in parallel to the conventional system. This in some respects has been bypassed and sometimes appears to resent the appearance on the scene of new upstart organization and institutions.

Most changes have taken place in the initial training of primary school teachers. Perhaps inevitably there has been less movement in terms of other kinds of post-initial training: the primary focus has meant that to a considerable extent the most powerful and authoritative teacher training agencies, the universities, have played a somewhat withdrawn role, leaving the initiative largely to governmental and official agencies. Perhaps this was inevitable, even desirable, and it is worth a few moments of further reflection.

THE UNIVERSITIES AND TEACHER EDUCATION

For many years we have argued the importance of the involvement of universities in teacher education. Only in universities were resources of expertise and knowledge sufficient to equip higher levels of the school system with the higher grade of product. Only in the universities could problem-oriented research be initiated and teacher education be infused with the most up-to-date findings of research. Only the universities could provide as part of their natural function the necessary international contacts and the filter through which international experience might be passed to ensure its relevance to the national situation.

To promote these wider functions we commonly established years ago institutes of education to work in association with university departments of education. The institutes carry out the specific tasks of research and development and feed stimulus and modernity into the school system through links with colleges of education and in-service training activities including provision for advanced and higher degree courses. But, as we have noticed in recent years, something rather odd appears to have happened. New agencies have come into existence to fulfill some of these tasks which we regarded as the university's field. New nonuniversity institutions have come into being, institutions that have attracted funding and have the capacity to undertake research, to conduct training programs, and even to consider offering degrees in some instances. National councils of one kind or another have been created to coordinate activities—research and college-based and in-service training, for example. Curriculum development centers and in some cases official "institutes" have taken over much of this work from universities. In some countries the significance of the university's role in teacher education must now be seriously questioned.

Why should this be? One important reason is that in countries striving for modernization and employing national development planning techniques, governments have a responsibility to control and direct in all areas of the national life including education, which is a vital engine of development. In consequence, the traditional autonomy of the university has, quite properly in my view, been challenged, although it has also in my view been reduced with counterproductive results. Some governments have been reluctant to work through universities claiming even a minimum of autonomy. They have been inclined to view student political activity and criticism from academics as a threat. Mutual suspicion between university staff and the political/official hierarchies has been a common and damaging fact of life in recent years. Consequently, universities have been deprived of the resources and the encouragement they need to make the kind of major impact upon educational systems that, as recently as ten years ago, we believed to be their responsibility.

At the same time universities have commonly contributed to the present situation. They have often focused their attention too narrowly upon the secondary education sector as indeed they were commonly encouraged to do in the early post–Addis Ababa years when the generation of high level manpower was thought to be our economic salvation. Universities often have been reluctant to involve themselves in primary or adult-oriented activities such as became the highest priorities in the 1970s. They were concerned to maintain the highest quality and standards of the international university world and consequently preferred to deal with relatively small numbers of students on conventional programs leading to conventional qualifications. They provided a valuable service in so doing, but they tended to neglect the development of more untidy, less satisfying programs of varying durations, leading to minor local qualifications or to none, and employing new techniques that might have contributed more immediately and directly to the solving of problems of education systems. A high proportion of the research effort of universities was directed to the achievement of higher degrees and career progression by staff, to the production of dissertations that now repose dusty and unread in the libraries, and too little to sustained and collaborative attacks on major problems too great to be handled by conventional individual research.

Once again, however, this gloomy picture must be qualified. These are the kinds of criticisms that have been heard about universities all over the world, including my own country. Reluctantly I personally have to concede that there is some justice in them, but I also have to note that a number of African universities have in various ways shown what can be achieved and that the spirit of innovation is far from dead.

In Nigeria I have long admired the flexibility with which Ahmadu Bello University has sought to respond to the training needs of the northern states through its TISEP program, and also through its more advanced Nigeria Certificate in Education by Correspondence program and its range of specialist diplomas and certificates. Ibadan University, too, through its part-time one-year Associateship Certificate in Education, has since 1979 offered upgrading courses to teachers in six states through a network of nine centers. An interesting feature of this program is that it is self-financing. Nsukka also offers the Advanced Certificate and the University of Lagos, through its program in professional studies in education, is currently offering sandwich courses to primary heads and inspectors in three curriculum areas. The Lagos Correspondence and Open Studies Unit is now moving from the provision of pre-university entry courses to diploma and degree programs.

The University of Zimbabwe is energetically introducing a two-year in-service postgraduate certificate program to replace its conventional residential course, and the University College of Botswana is launching a major primary education improvement project with a strong in-service component based on the master teacher principle. In Tanzania the university is to cooperate with the ministry and colleges of national education to provide a countrywide in-service program for teachers in secondary schools, teachers' colleges, and folk development colleges. More generally there has been a growth of first and higher degree programs to meet the career needs of qualified teachers. The Kenyatta University College Masters program for training tutors for primary teachers' colleges is particularly interesting.

No doubt other instances could be cited. Nevertheless it remains my view that in recent years leadership in teacher education has passed from the universities and that it is of vital importance for the health of African education systems that they re-establish themselves in the forefront of innovation at a time when innovation is still a lively growth. For I see in the current teacher education situation a series of somewhat sorrying dysjunctions.

Firstly, we find teacher education being undertaken by a bewildering range of agencies for an increasingly complex range of purposes: universities, government and voluntary agency colleges ranging from the advanced to the elementary, inspectorates and mobile teacher educators, curriculum development centers, resource and teachers' centers, teachers' unions, and professional associations. These agencies provide initial and upgrading, refresher and retraining programs, often overlapping and sometimes competing, rarely adequately coordinated and often lacking the conceptual framework that would permit planning decisions as to priorities and resource allocation.

Secondly, I see a disturbing survival of traditional dysjunctions between initial and in-service training, and between provision for primary and secondary education. These dysjunctions are of increasing significance in the context of mass education.

Thirdly, I see a distinct lack of convergence between educational research on the one hand and teacher education/curriculum and organizational development on the other. Here perhaps the most glaring deficiency in the field of teacher education is the general failure to apply objective research capacity to the cost effectiveness evaluation of the many alternative patterns of teacher education that I have been discussing. A further deficiency is the dearth of worthwhile studies relating to the management of educational innovation in African countries.

Fourthly, I see an increasing dysjunction between educationists of various nations, facing many problems in common, needing to draw upon each other's experience but often being unable to do so because that experience has too rarely been analyzed and recorded and because communication networks as they exist at present are still more likely to lead to London or New York than to neighboring countries in Africa and to countries in other parts of the developing world that have experience to share.

It is my contention that universities have a vital role to play alongside and in association with official organizations in overcoming some of these problems, not merely as one of many agencies involved in teacher education but more significantly as a source of new ideas; as a catalyst for new organizational patterns, techniques, and agencies; as an analyst and evaluator of patterns and programs; and as an agency whereby international experience may be sifted and communicated.

It is on this latter note that I wish to conclude. I am personally committed to the notion that educational progress must be enhanced by processes of cooperation, coordination, and sharing between and within nations. The success of the recently concluded INSET-AFRICA project,[12] a study of in-service education of primary school teachers in thirteen African countries, is sufficient proof in my eyes of the validity of my belief. This was a genuinely collaborative venture undertaken by representatives of fourteen national universities as well as my own, with a Ministry representative in the case of The Gambia. In designing this project I deliberately sought to place it under the aegis of the Association for Teacher Education in Africa. I did so because of my conviction that ATEA or a similar body has a vital role to play in promoting cooperation of the kind I have been discussing between teacher educators in African countries. As you know, ATEA has fallen upon hard times after many years during which its merits gradually came to be obscured by criticisms of it. I am conscious that it has weaknesses, among which I would include the fact that it was limited to institutional and to university membership, that recently it failed to generate action projects, and that it was too dependent upon external funding from the Carnegie Corporation. Yet it succeeded over a period of twenty years—as the Afro-Anglo-American Program for Teacher Education in Africa (AAA) and ATEA—in bringing together a whole generation of African teacher educators with some British and American colleagues, and in creating bonds of friendship and mutual respect between them, the value of which was undoubted though not possible to quantify. Those of us who were active participants will know the debt we owe for the opportunities to meet with leading colleagues from all parts of Africa and to discuss formally and informally our problems and projects. There could be no finer tribute to Karl Bigelow, whose vision, energy, and positive thinking on all issues contributed so greatly to the life of ATEA, than that active steps be taken to ensure that this kind of professional linkage is continued through the 1980s. And, as I have argued, at no time has such a linkage been more necessary than in the present exciting and more fluid circumstances.

NOTES

1. P. H. Coombs, *The World Educational Crisis: A Systems Analysis* (New York: Oxford University Press, 1968), p. 168.
2. D. E. Bell, *Report of the External Advisory Panel on Education to the World Bank* (Washington, D.C.: World Bank, 1978), p. 15.
3. A. R. Thompson, *Education and Development in Africa* (London: Macmillan, 1981).
4. N. D. J. Smart, "Teachers, Teacher Education and the Community," in R. Gardner, ed., *Teacher Education in Developing Countries: Prospects for the Eighties* (London: University of London Institute of Education, 1979).
5. Here I am using the typology of R. Chin and K. D. Benne as outlined in their "General Strategies for Effecting Change in Human Systems," in W. G. Bennis, K. D. Benne, R. Chin, and K. E. Corey, eds., *The Planning of Change* (New York: Holt, Rinehart and Winston, 1976).
6. UNESCO, *The Training of Educational Personnel: Report of a Regional Seminar, Chiangmai, Thailand, October, 1978* (Bangkok: UNESCO Regional Office for Education in Asia, 1979), pp. 7–8.
7. T. Husen, "Patterns and Structures for Teacher Education," in Gardner, *Teacher Education in Developing Countries*.
8. J. D. Turner, "Curriculum of Teacher Education," in Gardner, *Teacher Education in Developing Countries*.
9. T. Husen, "Patterns and Structures for Teacher Education."
10. H. W. R. Hawes, "The Curriculum of Teacher Education," in Gardner, *Teacher Education in Developing Countries*.
11. J. K. Nyerere, interview with David Martin, *New Internationalist* (May 1973), p. 7.
12. I have drawn extensively on the findings of the INSET-AFRICA project. Forthcoming publications will include national surveys of in-service education for primary teachers in Botswana (Ray Malomo), The Gambia (Pete Metuge), Ghana (K. Asiedu-Akrofi), Kenya (Henry Ayot), Liberia (Thomas Koon), Malawi (Joseph Mwale), Nigeria (Bukunola Osibodu), Sierra Leone (Adonis Labor), Swaziland (Bongile Putsoa),

Uganda (C. F. Oadaet), Zambia (Emmanuel Waddimba), and Zimbabwe (Doreen Sibanda). A synthesis study will be produced by Jeremy Greenland.
The following case studies will be published in the above:

Ray Malomo, "The Botswana In-Service Team: A Mobile Support Service for Primary Schools"

K. Asiedu-Akrofi, "The Ghana National Association of Teachers and the Professional Development of Teachers"

Henry Ayot, "Teacher Advisory Centres in Kenya"

Gerard Mathot, "The Lesotho In-Service Education for Teachers Programme"

Thomas Koon, "The Kakata Rural Teacher Training Institute in Liberia: Introducing Teachers to New Curricula"

Joseph Mwale, "The Domasi In-Service Centre in Malawi and Its Role in INSET"

Bukunola Osibodu, "The Part-Time Associateship Certificate in Education of the Institute of Education, University of Ibadan, Nigeria"

Uga Onwuka, "In-Service Teacher Training in the Four Eastern States of Nigeria: Four Case Studies"

Peter Lassa, "In-Service Teacher Training in the Ten Northern States of Nigeria: Four Case Studies"

Adonis Labor, "Government of Sierra Leone/EDF-Sponsored In-Service Teacher Education Programme for Untrained and Unqualified Teachers 1977–81"

Bongile Putsoa, "The William Pitcher College In-Service Department for the Upgrading and the Initial Training of Primary School Teachers in Swaziland"

C. F. Oadaet, " 'Initial' Training of Unqualified Teachers: Buloba Teacher Training College in Uganda"

Emmanuel Waddimba, "Zambia's Curriculum Development Centre and the In-Service Education of Teachers"

Doreen Sibanda, "The Zimbabwe Integrated Teacher Education Course"

Teacher Education in Africa: Modernization and Traditionalism Reconsidered

R. FREEMAN BUTTS

Teachers College, Columbia University

When I was first invited to deliver this lecture, I demurred for a time on the grounds that I had not been directly involved or closely following teacher education in Africa for the past six or seven years. Since my retirement from Teachers College in 1975 I had become so engrossed in fighting the educational battles in the United States that I had lost touch with the campaigns in Britain and Africa. But, then, I rationalized that perhaps there were some trends in the United States that could throw some light on our common struggles.

What really persuaded me was the chance to join this company again in discussions and conversations that would honor Karl Bigelow and what he so elegantly stood for. However, I do warn you at the outset that Karl and I were colleagues for nearly forty-five years and close friends for most of that time.

I arrived at Teachers College as a part-time teaching assistant in the fall of 1935 and was made a full-time instructor in September, 1936, just as Karl arrived as a visiting professor. Our mutual interests in the study of higher education brought us together. Very soon thereafter Karl went on leave to the General Education Board and then to the Commission on Teacher Education of the American Council on Educa-

---

Lecture delivered on March 1, 1982, at the Institute of Education, University of London.

tion. In fact, he tendered me my first offer of a job outside of Teachers College, inviting me to join him on the staff of the commission. But as I was just beginning to climb the academic ladder, I stayed at Teachers College and instead began to work in a new program in teacher education organized cooperatively by Teachers College, Columbia College, and Barnard College, under the auspices of Karl's commission.

We did keep closely in touch throughout his absence, and I took part in the commission workshops where I could admire Karl's professional leadership and enjoy his convivial company. Under his tutelage I learned the proper pronunciation of "rationale," and when the wandering discussion at a workshop session threatened to cut short his own prepared presentation, he could make the group enjoy the transition to a formal lecture by remarking, "There is no pain like the pain of an undelivered speech."

Upon his return to Teachers College in 1945, Karl plunged into various international activities with UNESCO and soon with special reference to Africa and African teacher education. It was nearly a decade before I caught his international fever, but still we were constantly caught up together in the academic affairs of Teachers College and also in faculty social affairs. Several couples joined together in a Sunday evening get-together that was at first called "The Morningside Heights Reading Aloud and Malt Liquor Society." But the cumbersome description of our agenda was soon shortened to "Masque and Bubbles," or just the "MB's." And when Karl was absent in Britain or Africa—away from his assigned dramatic roles at the MB reading aloud sessions—his letters would regale us with an almost hourly description of his international activities.

This background should put you on the alert concerning my perspective of Karl Bigelow as a colleague and friend. As it happened, however, it was not Karl who enticed me into international education. It was a Fulbright fellowship to Australia where in 1954 I was plunged into my first close and intensive study of a British-oriented educational system. I was there too short a time to write a long scholarly article and too long a time to write a "first impressions" travel book, so I had the presumption to settle for a short analytical report that probably revealed more about me and my shortcomings than it did about Australian education.[1] In any case it launched me into the rough seas of international education. For my pains I was put in charge of a committee planning the future role of international studies at Teachers College and, of course, Karl Bigelow was on the committee. I began to learn more intensely from *his* experience, but I myself had not yet touched Africa. While Karl spent 1958 at the London Institute, I was getting ready for another internship to British-oriented systems of education as manifested in India, where I launched a technical assistance project for Teachers College in 1958–1959. Mercifully, I did *not* write a book on Indian education, but some day I hope to look again at what I said in my reports for the succeeding nine years.

While I was busily engaged in trying to cope with large-scale technical assistance projects of Teachers College in Afghanistan and India, the Afro-Anglo-American (AAA) connections were being forged by John Lewis, John Wilson, Andy Taylor, and Karl Bigelow, with the enthusiastic intellectual and financial support of Alan Pifer and Steve Stackpole of the Carnegie Corporation of New York. This story is told in considerable and sympathetic detail in Pat Murphy's book on Carnegie and Africa.[2] And even if the personal and group conferences of these men were not made very public in 1958 and 1959, the principal actors were indeed giving intimations of their views to those who would read and listen.

In his inaugural lecture in the Institute of Education as professor of education with special reference to tropical areas, on February 5, 1959, John Lewis spoke on the theme "Partnership in Overseas Education." Not only did he refer to the earlier partnership of missions and government and universities in Africa, but more especially he looked forward to the kinds of partnership required for the improvement of education in the new and independent nations of Africa. In his final paragraphs he specifically mentioned American participation in the partnership of the future:

> There have been, and there still are people, sometimes influential persons, who suspect such American endeavour as being an expression of dollar imperialism. Such prejudice is without foundation and is detrimental to the establishment of a united world community. The tide of educational endeavour will eventually wash away such prejudice. Meanwhile, the co-operation which has existed in the past must be strengthened and extended. The educational needs of the new nations are such that the maximum of efficiency of effort is essential. That efficiency of effort will be attained if as in the past we see the responsibility for the study and extension of education in the new nations as an exercise in partnership.[3]

While John Lewis may have been somewhat overly optimistic about the disappearance of prejudice against American education, Karl Bigelow was affirming similar positive words concerning partnership in a paper he wrote when a visiting lecturer here in 1958: "Certainly we should thank our English friends for their testimony [about American education]. . . . We all labor in the same cause. We can learn from one another."[4]

Now I know that I shared these sentiments in the late 1950s. Belief that genuine partnership in international education was essential and that we could learn from one another was surely a basic reason why I had been drawn away from preoccupation with American education into the tides and currents of international education. But as I look back, I wonder if we were quite prepared for the problems and difficulties besetting mutual cooperation that boiled up in the crucibles within our three continents and in their interrelationships in the 1960s and 1970s. I shall come back to this point, but first I would like to explain how I got into this Afro-Anglo-American network of partnership to promote African teacher education.

Upon my return from India in 1959 I was made director of international studies at Teachers College. In this capacity I worked with Karl very closely on the developments that led to the Carnegie grant in May, 1960, in support of AAA, the idea being to promote cooperative efforts among African institutions, the Institute of Education, University of London, and Teachers College, through faculty exchanges, graduate fellowships for young African educators, joint research, and exchange of information. At Teachers College Karl was the prime mover as director of the program and as a member of the three-way AAA executive committee, along with John Lewis in London and Andy Taylor at Legon and at Ibadan.

This was the original tripod upon which was eventually built the Association for Teacher Education in Africa (ATEA) embracing more than thirty African institutions of teacher education. I eventually became a full-fledged participant in AAA and ATEA as the official representative of Teachers College, but before that time I went through an exceedingly strenuous period of induction and apprenticeship into the mysteries of British-oriented African education.

One day (or was it nighttime?) in December, 1960, Karl rang me up from Princeton, New Jersey, where he was attending a conference of the Africa Liaison Committee of the American Council on Education.

I shall never forget his introductory words: "J, I have a bear by the tail." That bear, it turned out, was an idea cooked up by Karl, Ralph Ruffner of the U.S. International Cooperation Administration (later USAID), and Bernard de Bunsen, principal of Makerere College in Kampala. Could Teachers College recruit, select, train, and deliver to East Africa 150 qualified secondary school teachers by July, 1961? My answer, "Well, ah, er, *yes.*" And Karl cheerfully handed that bear over to me.

Thus began the Teachers for East Africa project (TEA), a fairly small project as technical assistance in the 1960s was measured, but I happen to believe, in all modesty, one of the most successful, well planned, and effectively carried out examples of multilateral cooperation for the benefit of Third World development of the 1960s. The full story has never been fully investigated or told. It should be. What were its effects upon the thousands of African students who were touched by it, the hundreds of American, British, and African teachers who were involved during its relatively short life of almost a decade, and what were the ingredients of its success and its failures or inadequacies compared with other forms of international education? Some aspects of such queries have been studied, but an adequate research project would take at least as much cooperative and international effort as it took to launch and run the program.

But my point here today is that the groundwork of partnership established by the AAA was indispensable not only for the launching and administration of the TEA project involving six governments on three continents, a wide spectrum of educational, political, and economic ideologies in anticipation of independence for the East African countries, inevitable bureaucratic problems, and so on. AAA was also indispensable for helping to establish the fundamentally *professional* character of the TEA exercise in the face of the diverse claims and blames for the underdeveloped characteristics of the new nations.

In any case I shall always be thankful for the way paved for me in January and February, 1961, by AAA as my colleagues and I arrived in London and then visited in whirlwind fashion Uganda, Kenya, Tanganyika, and Zanzibar to see if such a project was not only needed but genuinely desired by the British authorities then in charge of London and in Africa, and even more importantly by the African authorities who would soon be in power in Africa.

I shall never forget a cold February day when I confronted John

Lewis in his office and asked him if we should mount the exercise. His answer: "You must." He didn't know me then; I suspect he had his doubts about this novice in African or indeed British educational affairs, but I also suspect that since I came with the imprimatur of Karl Bigelow, as I did, he thought I ought to be given a chance.

In any case, I arrived back in London with signed undertakings of the several African governments authorizing the project under joint British and American cooperation for financial support and for Teachers College to be the United States university to manage the project from the American side. I cannot detail the wide range of Britons and Africans who met with us personally in East Africa and assured us of the need for aid in supplying qualified secondary school teachers as well as giving assurances that professionally trained teachers from the United States would be welcome.

I do not know what has happened to most of the persons we dealt with on the trip, but one I know who is still in place is President Julius Nyerere himself. He not only welcomed us to the State House in Dar es Salaam in February, he came to Teachers College in July to greet the first batch of TEA teachers as they finished their orientation and were about to leave for East Africa. Another person who did the same thing that summer and who is still in place is W. Senteza Kajubi from Makerere University.

I arrived back in New York on the night of February 28, 1961, exhausted from the trip but happy to have those signed undertakings in my pocket to be presented in triumph to the officials of the United States technical assistance agency in Washington who had also acted with unprecedented speed. I woke up the next morning to read on the front page of the *New York Times* that President Kennedy had just created the Peace Corps under Sargent Shriver to send around the world thousands of young Americans, including teachers, to help nations both new and old that needed help in developing and modernizing themselves.

Despite a certain sinking feeling about what the Peace Corps might portend for TEA and a growing suspicion that the International Cooperation Administration in Washington may have acted so fast in order to put TEA in place before the Peace Corps could be established, or even to head it off, we pushed ahead with the program.

I believe, on balance, that my association with TEA was the most exhilarating and satisfying professional experience in my entire career.

For most of the persons involved, including myself, there was a special spirit of commitment and service and dedication to achieving a more humane and decent life for the newly independent peoples of the world. This spirit genuinely reflected the best of the Kennedy and the early Johnson years, and this spirit was dealt severe blows by the events and policies that marked the later 1960s and early 1970s. But aside from questions of spirit and affect, let me mention what we thought we were doing in more mundane terms.

I have elsewhere described the TEA as one of the most interesting and successful examples of American foreign aid policy stressing technical cooperation to aid in the human resource development of newly independent nations of Africa.[5] It reflected the growing recognition that education was an important element in national development. As the administrator of the reorganized Agency for International Development, David E. Bell, put it, "This is why we place so much emphasis on helping underdeveloped countries acquire skill and competence . . . to help establish institutions in the countries which can provide skilled, competent leadership for those countries, without outside help, as soon as possible."[6] And it reflected the undeniably documented fact that the greatest bottleneck preventing the development of leadership competence in the about-to-be-independent British territories of Kenya, Uganda, and Tanzania was the shortage of qualified secondary school teachers, made even more critical by the projected departure of British expatriate teachers upon the arrival of independence.

In the course of four years (1961–1965), 463 American college graduates were recruited, screened, selected, trained, and assigned to the secondary schools of East Africa where they served for two or more years as fully qualified education officers appointed by, paid by, and supervised by the professional officials of the newly independent African governments. The project officially ended in 1967.

The program had several major characteristics. It was based upon a genuine and demonstrable need in the receiving countries. It was based upon detailed cooperative planning and careful preparation among the British who were giving up authority, the Africans who were assuming authority, and the Americans who were being asked to assist in the transition (in fact, many new British teachers also became involved in the project). The teachers were carefully interviewed and selected to assure high professional qualifications as defined in the education codes

of the East African countries. The teachers were given specialized training to meet the particular conditions of teaching and pay required of
the educational services of the several African countries.

The TEA project differed substantially from the early Peace Corps
policies that put great stress upon the motives of volunteerism and the
values of "understanding other peoples" and providing needed skills on
a noncareer, temporary, emergency basis. In this view, specialized professional training or competence was not so important for teaching in
Africa as was the generalized liberal education of an American college
graduate. When it was decided in Washington in 1964 that the Peace
Corps would thereafter take over the task of providing American teachers to the countries of the world, serious objection was raised by the
governments of East Africa, by the British government, by AID-Wash-
ington, and by Teachers College. This was one of the most dishearten-
ing episodes in my African experience. I have in my files an eleven-page,
single-spaced typed memorandum signed by Karl and myself objecting
vigorously to the unilateral decision in Washington that we felt would
undercut the genuinely cooperative multilateral project that Africans,
British, and Americans had worked out.

We lost that battle and were faced with a special dilemma when
the East African governments told Washington that they would accept
Peace Corps volunteers to succeed TEA only if Teachers College trained
them. We had already trained Peace Corps volunteers for Sierra Leone,
Ghana, and Nigeria, and had had to fight battles with the Peace Corps
in order to devote greater emphasis to professional training beyond simply a general academic background and spirit of volunteerism. Upon further assurances from the new head of Peace Corps training, Joseph
Kaufman, that we could have a greater voice in designing the training
programs, we consented to the urgings of the British and East African
authorities. By the mid-1970s Teachers College had trained some 4,000
persons for educational service in Africa.

Teachers College not only trained Peace Corps volunteers for East
and West Africa but launched a significant but smaller program under
AID contract to provide tutors for the teacher training colleges of East
Africa (totaling 168 professionals, 1965–1972) who assisted in the training of primary as well as of secondary school teachers. In both cases the
immediate shortage of teachers was relieved, schools were kept open and
even expanded, Africanization was speeded up in the staffing of schools

and government positions, and in many instances the nature of the curriculum and teaching procedures was modified as well.

I must hasten to finish this part of my report to you, but I must add that the AAA/ATEA connection also enabled Teachers College to enter upon still another AID contract in 1972. This was a significantly new departure in technical assistance in that the agreement, initiated by the University of Lagos, was drawn up between the University of Lagos and Teachers College for developing a program to train tutors for teacher training colleges and supervisors in science and mathematics with a view to improving primary school instruction in those fields. The distinctive point was that it was a university-to-university agreement rather than a government-to-government contract. Despite its success, the AID funds dried up under the Nixon administration in the United States. A similar university-to-university effort between Teachers College and Makerere University withered as a result of the Amin administration in Uganda.

This brings me at last to my announced theme, a reconsideration of the idea of modernization and traditionalism. Here I speak only for myself and only from the perspective of the experiences I have had with the tripartite enterprise of British, American, and African collaboration in promoting teacher education in and for Africa. As I look back and reconsider the period from 1960 to 1975 while I was active in the affairs of the Afro-Anglo-American troika, I am impressed again by how often I found the rationale for the exercise in the idea of modernization that was being widely discussed in the political arena of Third World development as well as in the academic worlds of the West.[7]

CHARACTERISTICS OF A MODERNIZING SOCIETY

Let me summarize as briefly as I can what I came to identify as five general characteristics of a modernizing society.

A basic feature of modernizing societies is the mobilizing and centralizing power of the nation-state in relation to the other institutions of society: economic, religious, kinship, and voluntary. The process of rationalizing political authority into a single integrated policy designed to coordinate the centrifugal particularisms of locality, region, or pluralistic groups has been one of the most difficult yet characteristic aspects of the modernization process wherever it has occurred from the sixteenth century to the present. The more modern the society, the greater the capacity and the flexibility of the political system to influence the whole range of social and economic affairs of the society. The major agencies so often relied upon to achieve political community and nation-building are highly organized administrative and military bureaucracies, differentiated political structures designed to channel more effectively the legislative, executive, and judicial functions of the political system, and large-scale educational systems. Organized education has been called upon to provide the civic education that would socialize the populace to the values and attitudes required to maintain the political system, to help in the recruitment of its leaders, and to provide the professional training for those who manage the manifold institutions of a modern nation-state.

A second characteristic of modernizing societies is the increasing involvement of larger and larger numbers of people of all classes in political, economic, and social affairs. This trend was vastly accelerated by the revolutions that swept Europe and America in the eighteenth and nineteenth centuries and have swept Africa and Asia in the twentieth century. Whether the form of government be constitutional monarchy, representative democracy, socialism or communism, fascism or military dictatorship, mass participation in public affairs has become a means of mobilizing the populace into greater group efforts on behalf of the public good, however that might be defined. The entire political spectrum from left to right now pays more attention to the power of the people than ever before. And the political party, whatever form it might take, has become one of the distinctive institutional aspects or infrastructures of a modern society, whether it be based on the urban proletariat, peasants, middle classes, military or ruling elite; whether it be a genuine competitive system among several independent parties; or whether it be a single party limited to mass demonstrations, political rallies, and 99.9 percent affirmative votes in elections. Mass participation has often led to basic changes in access to education. In turn the prevalence of mass education has led to changes in the character of the participation.

A third characteristic of the transformation from a traditional to a modern society, and the one most commonly referred to as an attribute of modernization, is the shift from an agrarian society to a citified society; from subsistence agriculture and other primary means of production to commerce, the market system, and power-driven machine production in farm, factory, and city. These trends were related to mechanization and technical improvements in agriculture itself as well as to the growth of industrial urbanism; rural transformation, if not actually preceding industrialization, at least accompanied it.

Leadership in industrial modernization was sometimes exerted by capitalist entrepreneurs of the middle classes with cooperation from weak or minimal governments and sometimes by strong governments under the control of ruling elites directed by modern-minded monarchs, by military factions, or by socialist or communist parties. As the magnets of industrialization and urbanization continued to attract more and more people around the world, organized education has been intimately involved, sometimes helping to speed the process, sometimes holding it back, and sometimes being overwhelmed by it.

A fourth aspect of modernization may be summed up in the term secularization. Modern societies are peculiarly the inheritors of the scientific revolution in knowledge, initiated in the sixteenth and seventeenth centuries, accelerating in the eighteenth and nineteenth centuries, and exploding in the twentieth century. Secularization not only applies to the physical and natural sciences but also to the humanities, the social sciences, and the arts. It implies reliance upon rational methods of inquiry freed from the exactions of religious dogma, supernatural revelation, or mystical and personal insights not generally available. It applies not only to the systematic organization of knowledge for practical purposes in mechanical and industrial production, transportation, communication, and economic distribution based upon inventions and technical specialization, but also to the rational solving of problems in social and political affairs. The historian C. E. Black locates this reliance upon the application of scientific knowledge at the very heart of the modernization process:

> "Modernization" may be defined as the process by which historically evolved institutions are adapted to the rapidly changing functions that reflect the unprecedented increase in man's knowledge, permitting control over his environment, that accompanied the scientific revolution. This process of adaptation has its origins and initial influence in the societies of Western Europe, but in the nineteenth and twentieth centuries these changes have been extended to all other societies and have resulted in a worldwide transformation affecting all human relationships.[8]

The fifth characteristic of a modern society in contrast to a traditional society is a faith in and reliance upon organized systems of schooling available to ever increasing proportions of the population. Elaborate large-scale systems of organized education embracing a large part of the total population were something genuinely new under the sun, fashioned by modernizing societies, something that premodern societies had scarcely visualized let alone tried to establish. Organized public education was finely interwoven with the other strands of modernity just mentioned. It was an indispensable part of the means by which modernizing societies exerted their impact upon much of the rest of the world in the nineteenth and twentieth centuries.

I happen to think that this is still a useful way to describe deep-seated aspirations of many of the leaders of the new nations to overcome the gap between their own predominantly traditional societies and the more modern nations of the technologically developed world. Many of us in the West justified our technical assistance programs in education and in teacher education on the grounds that they would enable the new nations to modernize more effectively and quickly.

But as I look back I think I assumed too readily that *all* aspects of modernization were essentially desirable. I think I recognized the strength, complexities, and problems posed by the age-old traditional customs and values represented in the pluralisms of ethnic, religious, linguistic, racial, regional, and local loyalties. I know, and I think my writings show, that I did not put *economic* development as the sole or even the primary goal for educational assistance. As far back as 1962 I was stressing self-education of the newly independent nations as the primary goal of development or modernization.[9]

I was urging the educational planners of the new nations to promote five kinds of self-education: (1) education for economic development; I stressed even more (2) education for self-government; (3) education for a modern style of life that stressed dignity and self-respect, and the new identity of independence and freedom; (4) education for international responsibility in a growing interdependent world community; and (5) teacher education as the prime self-sustaining generator by which the new nations would produce their own teachers and not need to rely upon expatriate teachers. I sincerely believed then, and I believe now, that these were the basic goals of our tripartite efforts.

I now think that a flaw in the theory was to try to subsume all these good goals under the heading of modernization and to assume too easily that there were too few desirable values in some of the traditions of the African peoples whose leaders and planners were focusing on modernization. I do not refer simply to a needed emphasis upon African history, languages, art, music, dance, and literature. The imported colonial curriculum had indeed underplayed these aspects of African cultural life. I am wondering rather if there are themes or criteria by which to decide how to reconcile or reintegrate the values of traditional life with the values and pressures of modernization as these were imported from the West or adopted by African leaders.

HUMAN RIGHTS

Let me mention just one example, one of the most difficult and yet pervasive problems of the present era, the ideas and practices of basic human rights. It must be clear, or at least it is clear to me, that neither those nations devoted to modernization nor those devoted to traditionalism have a monopoly on dedication to human rights, say, as spelled out in the United Nations Universal Declaration of Human Rights of 1948, or the International Covenant on Civil and Political Rights of 1976. The Shah of Iran's drive to modernize was accompanied by violations of human rights that helped traditionalists to overthrow his regime, but his successors seem to be no more committed to freedom, privacy, due process, or justice in the meaning of the declaration or the covenant than was the Shah. Governments from the left to the right, from the military rulers of Communist Poland to the military rulers of Chile, trample on human rights when they deem it necessary.

You will note that these examples are *not* taken from African states. I shall venture only one example from Africa and limit that one to authors I can quote to make my point about distinguishing between desirable and undesirable aspects of traditional values. In a very interesting volume on human rights and the Third World, Dunstan Wai from the Southern Sudan has a chapter on "Human Rights in Sub-Saharan Africa." In his conclusion he says:

> The analytical survey presented in the preceding pages shows clearly that there was respect for human rights in traditional African societies but that colonialism imposed authoritarian institutions upon them and destroyed any meaningful popular participation in traditional decision-making processes. . . .

This study also shows that the record of human rights practices in tropical Africa has not been impressive. African politicians
and scholars are concerned about the issue of human rights, as evi-
denced by their policy pronouncements and participation in international conferences on the subject. But those who are in power
commit the same violations of human rights as did their predeces-
sors. Rationalizations of African authoritarian systems do not stand
up to close intellectual scrutiny as they are morally indefensible.[10]

Here then is one line of argument that finds positive value in the tradition of human rights based upon participation in decision-making and
the rule of law in traditional African politics, a tradition that was undermined by the colonial denial of popular participation by African
people.

Another view that finds deplorable elements in African traditionalism is that of Ali Mazrui, a former professor at Makerere and adviser
to Idi Amin. He describes Amin as an example of the paradox of heroic
evil: he was at once viewed as a hero by much of the Third World for
his defiance and confrontation with the North, and as a villain because
of the tyranny and anarchy he loosed upon the people of Uganda.[11] Ali
Mazrui views much of the centrally-directed force and brutal wanton
violence that afflicted Uganda under Amin as arising from ethno-
cultural-religious hostilities and animosities deeply embedded in the
tribal and community groups of Uganda. This is quite another view of
traditionalism. As with modernization so with traditionalism—all is not
good or bad. When the lights went out under Amin, the norms and
values attached to human rights came abruptly to an end.

What then is the meaning of all this for teacher education in
Africa? I will venture one kind of answer. I believe that it is not enough
to stress the need for modernization alone nor simply the need for re-
asserting African cultural traditions in the curriculum. Somehow dis-
tinctions should be made that put emphasis upon those elements in
both modernization and traditionalism that contribute to an understanding and commitment on the part of teachers and students alike to
basic human rights. It is in this realm that I believe my views of the
1960s were inadequate. If I may say so, I believe that this is also true of
much of the deliberation of the AAA and ATEA conferences.

I know that conferences and statements spoke recurrently of the
need for attention to the "social role of the future teacher"[12] (Bill
Dodd); that "the competent teacher must be educated to see and inter-

pret the needs of the country"[13] (J. G. Kiano); that teacher education should be "basically related to every phase of development"[14] (A. Babatunde Fafunwa); that every teacher needs "knowledge and understanding of the society to which he belongs"[15] (John Lewis); and that educators in Africa need to "promote attitudes in school which are aimed at solving the major problems facing the continent"[16] (W. Senteza Kajubi).

This was a major theme of a meeting held at the Institute of Education in May, 1975, to review the education policy of the World Bank. The meeting was led by Reg Honeybone and Peter Williams. Among the many aspects of the World Bank's report that were criticized, Peter Williams especially pointed out that despite the bank's references to the "social dimensions" of development it really stressed economic development through knowledge and skills:

> The paper appeared very largely to ignore the role of education in the promotion of social attitudes and values and in relation to the culture and religion of a community.[17]

Jeremy Greenland took up Williams's point that the "social dimension" was defined too narrowly and preoccupied with the economic functions of education. He too argued that:

> The development process was intimately bound up with social and cultural values and with the moral, ethical and religious domain of the curriculum. UNESCO and foreign advisers, upon whom the poorest countries generally relied for advice, naturally fought shy of involvement in this area. Thus the quite erroneous view gained ground that curriculum was basically a technical matter concerned with economically useful knowledge and skills, rather than with cultural attitudes, beliefs and values and with social relationships.[18]

If I had been at the meeting I would have heartily agreed with these sentiments. I would probably even have tried to expand the social dimension to include political values as I was beginning to do in the United States with respect to American education. That, indeed, may have been premature then and perhaps it still is, but I think we should look again at the questions.

As it was, ATEA had already begun to get down to the business of drawing up a book of readings for courses in foundations of education that would enable teacher educators to bring scholarship and disciplined inquiry to the social dimension. As a result of papers read and discussions conducted at the Monrovia Conference in 1970 and the Kampala Conference in 1971, a group of us under the able leadership of E. Ayotunde Yoloye and S. N. Nwosu put together two volumes of readings in the *Foundations of African Education*.[19] I remind you of the themes: Volume I was entitled "The Drive to National Unity and Identity"; Volume II, "The Drive to Modernization." These two themes at once reveal the major emphases I have been talking about. They were indeed uppermost in our minds in the 1960s. But now I believe we need a third volume to take account of what we have all been through in the 1970s. I suggest that the theme be something like "The Drive for Civic Learning and International Human Rights."

I cannot recite the history of events in our several countries in the decade of the 1970s that have undermined or weakened the cohesive political ties that make orderly and humane governance possible: Vietnam and Watergate in the United States; growing unrest and disturbances arising from ethnic and religious conflict in Britain; successions of military coups, civil wars, and tribal conflicts in several African countries. As for me, I have been concentrating much of my attention since 1975 to the task of trying to revitalize civic education in the schools and colleges of the United States.[20] I note that a parallel if not similar movement has been going on here under the tutelage of Bernard Crick, Alex Porter, Ian Lister, Derek Heater, Garth Allen, and others to promote political education and political literacy in secondary schools and colleges of further education.[21]

I do not know whether there have been comparable developments in African countries, but it seems to me that the theme of international human rights is one that our tripartite approach could most valuably and appropriately deal with in the future. The world now has a kind of value consensus hammered out through the United Nations in the late 1960s and early 1970s and deposited in the International Covenant on Civil and Political Rights (March, 1976), in the International Covenant on Economic, Social and Cultural Rights (January, 1976), and in the UNESCO agreement with the formidable title "Recommendation Concerning Education for International Understanding, Co-operation and Peace and Education Relating to Human Rights and Fundamental Freedoms." I strongly urge study of the book by Thomas Buergenthal and Judith V. Torney, *International Human Rights and International Education*.[22]

I know that many differences still remain between the East and West and between the North and South as to what these rights mean and how they should be realized or enforced. The North is likely to stress civil and political rights; the South, economic and social, but I believe that they provide the most important agenda for cooperative analysis and discussion for teacher educators in all of our countries for the 1980s. I propose that we start with the civil and political rights to see how far we can achieve a sense of shared values regarding the meaning of the basic concepts of justice, freedom, equality, diversity, authority, privacy, participation, and due process. I believe we could learn a great deal from each other regarding ways that schools and universities can or cannot promote these values.

I quite realize that research studies on political socialization and education for political values in African schools conducted in the 1960s by Kenneth Prewitt, George Von der Muhll, David Koff, and the work of David Court and others were not very optimistic about what Uganda schools were doing or could do. Prewitt and Okello Oculi argued:

> Necessary, though not sufficient, conditions for programmed political education are a doctrine and a means of transmitting it. Uganda does not meet these preliminary conditions. Neither doctrine, administrative structures, teaching materials, nor teachers have been adequately marshalled to the task of citizenship training or political indoctrination.[23]

I am not proposing "programmed political education" or "political indoctrination," but I am proposing that all of our countries could profitably work on formulating the "doctrine" (human rights), creating "teaching materials" that enable students to face realistically and with scholarly help the basic concepts underlying human rights; and constructing courses in teacher education that prepare teachers as citizens in order to enable them to help their students to be citizens devoted to human rights in their nation and in the world.

Many new projects are under way in the United States to try to improve civic learning. One that I know best and one that I think is the best is called Law in a Free Society.[24] Curriculum materials from kindergarten through high school have been developed dealing with such fundamental concepts as justice, authority, responsibility, privacy, freedom, participation, diversity, and property.

I am struck by the similarity of these concepts with some of those outlined by Bernard Crick in the British project on political literacy. Also, both approaches overlap in many respects with the basic human rights embodied in the UN and UNESCO formulations that are no longer to be identified with the West but represent aspirations of peoples and nations all over the world. What fascinating comparative studies could be made of the way such concepts and ideas might be treated in the schools and teacher educating institutions of our several countries.

I come back to Ali Mazrui:

> The world has found that it is not enough to destroy a tyrant. The successful action against Amin must now be accompanied by a dedication to the reconstruction of the society which produced him. It is easy enough to preach human rights. It is far more difficult to practice human partnership. Uganda is one compelling test for all concerned. . . . The "New International Moral Order" requires therefore at least three levels of conscience: the conscience of the individual, be that person ruler or subject; the conscience of each society, be that society powerful or weak; and the conscience of the world community as a whole.[25]

What all this means to me is that somehow we must indeed "decolonize modernization without stopping it,"[26] but at the same time we must humanize it. This modernization cannot mean a simple exportation of "democracy" from America or from the West to nations that are not ready for it because of their cultural or political traditions. But surely it must include at the very least the shared values of personal liberty, due process, and the rule of law. As S. M. Lipset, president of the American Political Science Association, put it nearly 20 years ago:

> Clearly the odds are against democracy in the new states of Africa and Asia. Many experts on these countries suggest that democracy may be a utopian short-term objective for such nations. Instead of speaking generally about democracy, it may be advisable to focus on the conditions which protect personal liberty, that is, on due process and the rule of law. Perhaps we should ask as we look at new countries: under what circumstances is a post-revolutionary regime, or the government of a new state, compatible with the rule of law?[27]

I would add: What kind of education will serve to maintain and promote the rule of law?

RESPONSE TO REVISIONISM

I have been suggesting some ways in which the framework of modernization I adopted in the 1960s might be modified for the 1980s, but now I would like to conclude by defending it from the critique of a latter day leftist revisionism that has grown up in the 1970s, just as I was leaving the field. I refer to a complex mixture of views that describe American technical assistance programs of governments, foundations, and university programs as basically "neo-colonialist" and "cultural imperialist" in motivation and practice. The works in the United States of Philip Altbach, Martin Carnoy, Gail Kelly, Edward Berman, Irving Spitzberg, and Robert Arnove illustrate these views.[28]

They argue that the real designs and effects of technical assistance have been to export educational ideas and institutions that would replace the old colonialism of political domination over the Third World with cultural and educational domination. This was done in order to continue an intellectual hegemony over the newly educated elites of Africa and Asia and keep them in a state of dependency upon American and Western liberal, capitalist, exploitative society. Of particular interest here has been the exportation and influence of Western university institutions and American philanthropic foundations.

Three quotations must suffice to indicate these views, especially as related to the enterprises I have been discussing. Altbach and Kelly make the general point about cultural neocolonialism this way:

Most Third World countries find that they cannot, without major social revolution, depart from education structures of the past. . . . They also find that, as they expand and develop their educational systems, they become as dependent as they were during the time of direct foreign rule on the educational goods and services of foreigners. . . . This has meant that school texts, books, curriculum, language of instruction, and even school teachers are imported from abroad and are accountable not primarily to the parents of students or to Third World nations but in part to either the United States, French, Soviet, Dutch or British governments or the Ford, Rockefeller, or Carnegie foundations.[29]

Arnove uses Marxist arguments underlying cultural imperialism and the concept of ideological hegemony to describe the role of American philanthropic foundations:

> A central thesis is that foundations like Carnegie, Rockefeller, and Ford have a corrosive influence on a democratic society; they represent relatively unregulated and unaccountable concentrations of power and wealth which buy talent, promote causes, and in effect, establish an agenda of what merits society's attention. They serve as "cooling-out" agencies, delaying and preventing more radical structural change. They help maintain an economic and political order, international in scope, which benefits the ruling-class interests and philanthropists and philanthropoids—a system which, as the various chapters document, has worked against the interests of minorities, the working class, and Third World peoples.[30]

Ed Berman delivered a specific coup de grace aimed directly at the Carnegie Corporation and Teachers College because of their joint efforts to manipulate AAA and TEA in their own interests. That is, he says, they were jointly designed to promote American foreign policy objectives in Africa and bind the newly independent African nations to the United States by funding programs that linked the educational systems of the new African nations to the values, modus operandi, and institutions of the United States. Although our public rhetoric pointed to nonpolitical technocratic support to help Africa modernize, our private papers and documents suggest that:

> This public rhetoric of disinterested humanitarianism was little more than a facade behind which the economy and strategic interests of the United States have actively been furthered . . . particularly with respect to the vested economic interests of the United States corporate and financial sectors.[31]

According to Berman, one of the important culprits in this campaign to maintain the cultural dependence of the new African states was the AAA and the chief perpetrators were Alan Pifer, John Lewis, and Karl Bigelow. Berman makes passing reference to TEA, though not by name, by saying: "The awarding of this contract to Teachers College was a way of assuring that change in East Africa, at least that occurring through the educational system, would not be revolutionary."[32]

The footnote to this sentence reads in part: "The Teachers College approach to educational change in developing nations was identical to that of the funding agencies themselves, i.e., gradual, moderate, and controllable. Details can be gleaned from a perusal of the Bigelow papers at Teachers College."[33]

I am tempted to say at the outset that apparently Ed Berman would have preferred that our approach had been revolutionary, abrupt, immoderate, and uncontrollable. But I do not dismiss the revisionist views out of hand. I believe they need to be considered carefully and examined with the most careful scholarship and analysis. I have no doubt that there were political and foreign policy motivations in the American technical assistance programs that began on a large scale with the Marshall Plan following the war. The predominance of military and economic aid reflected this fact, but the growth of education and teacher education in technical assistance was a different matter in the hands of men like David Bell and Harlan Cleveland and of many of the AID people with whom I worked for fifteen years in TEA and Teacher Education for East Africa (TEEA), in Nigeria, India, Afghanistan, and Peru.

Regarding the specific charges just stated, I categorically reject the revisionist presumption and argument insofar as they apply to the relationships of the Carnegie Corporation and Teachers College as I personally and professionally took part in AAA and ATEA from 1960 to 1975. I can do little more than state this view publicly today, but I invite the closest kind of analysis of my published writings during the fifteen-year period and also of my unpublished papers, some of which I turned over to my successors at Teachers College and are now in the files of the Office of International Services and the Institute of International Studies, and some of which (perhaps the most interesting) are now or soon will be in the archives of the Hoover Institution of Stanford University in California where I now live.

I sincerely wish that a series of full-scale research studies representing the three-way perspectives of British, African, and American scholars and ranging across a spectrum of orientations from left, liberal, and right could be conducted with regard to the relationships of Anglophone Africa, Britain, and the United States in the realm of teacher education in the 1960s and 1970s.

In addition to poring over the files in our several institutions and governments, what a record might be compiled by follow-up studies of the roles played in the national development of their countries by the thousands of students who attended the primary and secondary schools, teacher training colleges and universities in Africa where African, British, and American teachers were working together from 1961 onward for more than a decade. What happened to and what roles have been played by the British and Americans after their return from Africa? Did those Africans who came to Teachers College for graduate study turn out to be coopted elites working on behalf of American corporate interests in their respective countries? I think I understand something of the difficulties of such research and perhaps some of it has already been done, but what better way to make sound judgments concerning what I believe to have been a most significant episode of multinational cooperation?

Certainly we made mistakes, blunders, and bumbles. We had our disagreements, misunderstandings, and conflicts. I discovered in my files confidential notes I made as I visited fifty-two of the first sixty-two American teachers posted to East African schools in October and November, 1961. I am amazed what fascinating reading they make after twenty years. In general, I thought they were doing exceedingly well according to their own testimony, that of their headmasters, colleagues, and students, and my own observations of them in their homes and classrooms.

There were problems, of course, but surprisingly few major difficulties in the realm of teaching and academic preparation. Problems arose out of differing attitudes toward personal and social relationships of the tripartite staff. Often remarked by the Americans were the reserve, aloofness, and formality of the Britons, and by the Britons the overly aggressive and talkative informality, and especially the English usage, of the Americans, and not all African staff members quickly warmed up to the Americans, somewhat to their surprise.

While such matters loomed large in some minds at that time, the point I would make here is what Prime Minister Julius Nyerere emphasized in his talks with me in Mwanza and in Dar es Salaam, namely, that the TEA teachers were not only helping to speed up the Africanization of the educational system at the administrative level but also the public service of other branches of the government. How was this? The TEA teachers kept the classrooms open and enabled trained African teachers to move into responsible administrative posts without closing the schools.

Some of the revisionists sound as though they think it would have been better to close the schools and start over. Instead, we saw our job to be not to run the schools nor even to teach in the schools for long, but to make it possible for the East African countries to run their own schools and train their own teachers. As this was made possible, the Africans could then decide what kind of schools and what kind of teachers they wanted. I simply do not believe that Africans were brainwashed to maintain the British system or to adopt the American system. One guarantee of this was that African teacher educators were increasingly exposed to the educational ideas of different parts of the First and Second as well as the Third Worlds, and to the exchange of ideas among the several African countries themselves—two tasks that I believe AAA and ATEA effectively promoted.

Perhaps the Africanization of AAA was not as rapid as it might have been. I know that some Africans felt so, and if Ed Berman only knew it, Steve Stackpole of Carnegie and I from Teachers College were among those who, along with W. Senteza Kajubi and some other Africans, were pushing for speedier action, especially from the Isle of Thorns Conference in 1965 onward. By 1969 the Africans had taken full charge of the exercise, and not long afterward London Institute and Teachers College became *associate* members of ATEA, moving from the center to the periphery in less than a decade, something that could not happen in the revisionists' lexicon.

But I believe that in the last analysis the best guarantee against the doctrine of "penetration and dependency," of "neocolonial hegemony," and of "cultural imperialism" was the pervasive spirit with which so many of us from Britain and the United States undertook the task. This was no facade to mask ulterior designs. I believe it was best expressed by one of our first TEA teachers, Nathanial Frothingham III, a graduate of Harvard and Makerere, who wrote back to Harvard from Alliance High School, Kikuyu, Kenya, in April, 1962:

> There is an immense need for education. There is a need for teachers. . . . The young men whom I teach will take important positions in government and in the service of their country and peoples. Nothing gives me more pleasure than knowing that I am contributing to their education and that the impact of their lives will have profound effects upon the future of these lands. . . . I am not an instrument of political persuasion. I hope that my stu-

dents will learn to think and be free. They must arrive at answers
for what best suits their individual and unique destiny. This is why
the mission is delicate and sensitive.[34]

Please note how close this view, written from Kenya in 1962, is to
that of Alan Pifer who, as president of Carnegie, wrote in response to
Berman in 1979:

> If there was an explicitly articulated motivation behind Carnegie
> Corporation's work in Africa at that time . . . it was to produce
> African leaders who had the independence of mind and the vision
> to hold themselves aloof both from slavish adherence to inherited
> British educational forms and from uncritical adoption of the
> American model and to consider *de novo* what kind of education
> would best meet Africa's needs. . . . There was . . . a body of
> far-sighted and large-spirited people, British and American, of
> whom L. J. Lewis of London University and Karl Bigelow of Teach-
> ers College, Columbia, were typical, whose only thought was to
> help African nations build new educational systems suitable for
> *their* needs. Such people, and the Africans they identified and
> trained to be the leaders of the future, were the ones Carnegie
> Corporation sought out and supported. I am grateful to Mr. Ber-
> man for creating the opportunity for me to say publicly how proud
> I am of that record.[35]

I am happy to be able to say publicly how glad I am to have been
associated with those large-spirited and far-sighted people and this enterprise, as I hope my remarks today have attested.

CONCLUSION

One last word. The final ATEA meeting that I attended was the
dinner in Nairobi on March 28, 1975. The plan was for several of us
to take part in the after-dinner speeches, marking as it did the retire-
ments of Steve Stackpole and myself. Somehow the extended remarks
of others, not unusual for ATEA conferences, did not leave time for my
response before I had to rush to catch the plane to New York. But I
have just turned up some notes I had prepared for that response. So now
I have my chance. I would have said something like this:

At this morning's session I looked back over my fifteen years in and with Africa. This evening I would like to look ahead. I predict that in the next fifteen years the idea of ATEA will take hold and our membership will have expanded even beyond Africa. When we meet here in Nairobi in 1990 we will be under the auspices of an ATEA to which has been added several A's and E's (assuming that we will be as bound to those two letters of the alphabet as we have been in the past). So it will be the ATEAAEAAE, the Association for Teacher Education in Africa, America, Europe, Asia, Australia (Antarctica?) and finally E for Ecumene. Thus we will have been the nucleus of an association to improve teacher education throughout the world devoted to genuinely mutual collaboration and research. We shall have become a genuine "teaching college for the world" which I had grandly envisioned at the very outset of TEA.

In addition to this grandiose hope I would like to allude to the changes in the context of development assistance that have occurred in the early 1970s. For example, the headlines of March, 1975, report that Saudi Arabia is seeking U.S. academic help and Nigeria is seeking teachers from the U.K. and the U.S.A., and both are trying to figure out how to spend the enormous wealth produced by their oil. I have a suggestion for them, a new form of development assistance to aid both partners, summed up in our usual letters of the alphabet, ATAT = A Teacher for a Tanker.

But on a more sober note I do express another hope, this time symbolized by an acronym HOPE itself and embracing what I have tried to convey to the successive waves of teachers and tutors we have sent to Africa. My hope is that ATEA will continue to promote modernization in the new nations of Africa that is:

Humane
   • based on civil, political, and human rights;
   • not oppressive, exploitative, brutal, or cruel.
Open
   • based on freedom, diversity, self-government, pluralism;
   • not secretive, conspiratorial, confining.
Peaceful
   • based on reason, negotiation, planning, the rule of law;
   • not violence, terrorism, or war.
Educational
   • through self-education to develop the potentials of all the people, so that they may achieve a sturdy and stable nationhood, a satisfying modernity, genuine freedom, justice, and equality, and an international comity.

Let our motto be: Where there is ATEA there is HOPE. And I have one final hope—that I'll be seeing you all later.

Today I have been granted the privilege of satisfying part of that final hope by being able to see so many of you again at this reunion. And, not least, I have finally been relieved of the pain of an undelivered speech that has been waiting for seven years to be delivered! I thank you all for making that possible.

I cannot close this speech without just a touch of "reading aloud" which I think Karl would have liked. At least he heard me read it a good many times to those waves of teachers we sent to Africa in what I liked to call a "teaching college for the world." I take it from John Masefield's fond recall of his youthful days here in Bloomsbury, but it could just as well apply to AAA and ATEA when we gathered on Morningside Heights or Makerere Hill or any of the other campuses where we convened:

O Time, bring back those midnights and those friends,
Those glittering moments that a spirit lends. . . .
Those hours of stricken sparks from which men took
Light to send out to men in song or book. . . .
The glory of mood where human frailty failed,
The forts of human light not yet assailed,
Till the dim room had mind and seemed to brood
Binding our wills to mental brotherhood,
Till we became a college, and each night
Was discipline and manhood and delight,
Till our farewells and winding down the stairs
At each grey dawn had meaning that Time spares
That we, so linked, should roam the whole world round
Teaching the ways our brooding minds had found
Making that room our Chapter, our one mind
Where all that this world soiled should be refined.[36]

NOTES

1. R. Freeman Butts, *Assumptions Underlying Australian Education* (Melbourne: Council for Educational Research, 1955, and New York: Teachers College, Columbia University, 1955).

2. E. Jefferson Murphy, *Creative Philanthropy: Carnegie Corporation and Africa, 1953–1973* (New York: Teachers College Press, 1976).
3. L. J. Lewis, *Partnership in Overseas Education*, Studies in Education, no. 9, University of London Institute of Education (London: Evans Brothers, 1959), p. 23.
4. Karl W. Bigelow, "Some British Views on American Education," *Teachers College Record* 60, no. 7 (April 1959): 377.
5. For my own early analysis to 1963, see R. Freeman Butts, *American Education in International Development* (New York: Harper and Row, 1963), chapter 3.
6. Ibid., p. 26.
7. For the modernization theme as I viewed it, see, for example, such subsequent titles as:

   "The African University and Human Resource Development: An Educationist's View" in the volume of papers presented at the Lake Mohonk Conference on the African University of National Educational Development sponsored by the Afro-Anglo-American Program for Teacher Education in Africa and the Institute for African Education, Teachers College, Columbia University, September 8–18, 1964. Excerpts published in John W. Hanson and Cole S. Brembeck, eds., *Education and the Development of Nations* (New York: Holt, Rinehart and Winston, 1966), pp. 372–381.

   "A Teaching College for the World," delivered at the annual convocation of "Frontiers of Educational Thought," School of Education, Indiana University, November 13, 1964; published as Occasional Paper no. 65–103, October, 1965, Center for the Study of Educational Policy, School of Education, Indiana University.

   "Civilization as Historical Process: Meeting Ground for Comparative and International Education," *Comparative Education* (Oxford: Pergamon Press) 3, no. 3 (June 1967): 155–168.

   "Civilization-Building and the Modernization Process: A Framework for the Reinterpretation of the History of Education," *History of Education Quarterly* 7, no. 3 (Summer 1967): 147–174.

   "Teacher Education and Modernization," in George Z. F. Bereday, ed., *Essays on World Education* (New York: Oxford University Press, 1969), pp. 111–132, originally a working paper for the International Conference on the World Crisis in Education, held at Williamsburg, VA, October 5–9, 1969.

   "America's Role in International Education: A Perspective on Thirty Years," chapter 1 in National Society for the Study of Education

68th Yearbook, *The United States and International Education* (Chicago: University of Chicago Press, 1969), pp. 3–45.

"Reconstruction in Foundation Studies: Touchstone for Curriculum Reform in Teacher Education," *Educational Theory* 23, no. 1 (Winter 1973): 27–41; keynote address at the annual conference of the Association for Teacher Education in Africa, Makerere University, Kampala, Uganda, March 29, 1971.

"New Futures for Comparative Education," *Comparative Education Review* 17, no. 3 (October 1973): 289–294.

The Education of the West: A Formative Chapter in the History of Civilization (New York: McGraw-Hill, 1973), parts 3 and 4.

Public Education in the United States, From Revolution to Reform (New York: Holt, Rinehart and Winston, 1978), parts 2 and 3.

8. C. E. Black, *The Dynamics of Modernization; A Study in American History* (New York: Harper and Row, 1966), p. 7.

9. R. Freeman Butts, *American Education in International Development*, chapter 4.

10. Dunstan M. Wai, "Human Rights in Sub-Saharan Africa," in Adamantia Pollis and Peter Schwab, eds., *Human Rights; Cultural and Ideological Perspectives* (New York: Praeger, 1979), pp. 127–128. See also his discussion of "Human Rights in Africa" in Rockefeller Foundation Working Papers, *Human Rights, Human Needs, and Developing Nations* (New York: Rockefeller Foundation, 1980), pp. 43–63.

For a somewhat different African view see Jack L. Nelson and Vera M. Green, eds., *International Human Rights: Contemporary Issues* (Stanfordville, NY: Human Rights Publishing Group, 1980). In his chapter on "The African Perspective," Chris C. Mojekwu, an Eastern Nigerian, points to the precolonial role of human rights in Africa which the colonialists did not understand or appreciate, but he stresses the fact that those human rights rested heavily on ascribed status in a group and were based upon communal or collective rights rather than individual rights: "Citizenship and nationality were based on kinship communities founded on common culture, language, custom, and religion-ethnicity. Only those who 'belonged' to the community would have their human rights protected by the kinship authorities. . . . When, therefore, the U.N. principle of self-determination was transformed into universal human rights for the individual, it went counter to the African concept of human rights, which is communal" (pp. 93, 92).

11. Ali A. Mazrui, "Between Development and Decay: Anarchy, Tyranny and Progress Under Idi Amin," *Third World Quarterly* 2, no. 1 (January 1980): 44–58.

12. W. A. Dodd, *Teacher Education in the Developing Countries of the Commonwealth: A Survey of Recent Trends* (London: Commonwealth Secretariat, 1970).

13. Kenya Institute of Education, *New Directions in Teacher Education* (Nairobi: Africa Publishing House, 1969), p. xv.

14. Ibid., p. 84.

15. Ibid., p. 63.

16. P. C. C. Evans, ed., *Report of the Sixth Annual Conference of the Afro-Anglo-American Programme* (Oxford: Alden Press, 1968), p. 42.

17. Peter Williams, ed., *Prescription for Progress? A Commentary on the Education Policy of the World Bank* (London: University of London Institute of Education, 1976), p. 74.

18. Ibid., p. 88.

19. E. Ayotunde Yoloye and S. N. Nwosu, eds., *Foundations of African Education*, 2 vols., prepared for the Western Regional Council of the Association for Teacher Education in Africa.

20. The summation of much of my writing on civic education since 1973 is included in *The Revival of Civic Learning: A Rationale for Citizenship Education in American Schools* (Bloomington, IN: Phi Delta Kappa Educational Foundation, 1980).

21. Bernard Crick and Alex Porter, *Political Education and Political Literacy* (London: Longmans, 1978). See also Garth Allen, "Researching Political Education Programmes in Schools and Colleges," *International Journal of Political Education* 2 (1979): 67–82, 141–156.

22. See, especially, Thomas Buergenthal and Judith V. Torney, *International Human Rights and International Education* (Washington, D.C.: U.S. National Commission for UNESCO, 1976). This volume includes major documents on human rights in addition to analysis of them. See also F. E. Dowrick, ed., *Human Rights: Problems, Perspectives and Texts* (Durham, England: University of Durham, 1979).

23. Kenneth Prewitt, ed., *Education and Political Values: an East African Case Study* (Nairobi: East African Publishing House, 1971), pp. 12–13.

24. Law in a Free Society, a project of the Center for Civic Education established by and affiliated with the State Bar of California, 5115 Douglas Fir Drive, Calabasas, CA 91302.

25. Mazrui, "Between Development and Decay," pp. 57–58.

26. Ali A. Mazrui, "The African University as a Multinational Corporation: Problems of Penetration and Dependency," *Harvard Educational Review* 43, no. 2 (May 1975): 192.

27. Seymour Martin Lipset, *The First New Nation: The United States in Historical and Comparative Perspective* (New York: Basic Books, 1963), p. 11.

28. See, for example, Martin Carnoy, *Education as Cultural Imperialism* (New York: David McKay, 1974); Philip G. Altbach and Gail P. Kelly, *Education and Colonialism* (New York: Longman, 1978); Irving J. Spitzberg, Jr., ed., *Universities and the International Distribution of Knowledge* (New York: Praeger, 1980); and Robert F. Arnove, ed., *Philanthropy and Cultural Imperialism: The Foundations at Home and Abroad* (Boston: G. K. Hall, 1980).

29. Altbach and Kelly, *Education and Colonialism*, p. 41.

30. Arnove, *Philanthropy and Cultural Imperialism*, p. 1.

31. Edward H. Berman, "Foundations, United States Foreign Policy, and African Education, 1945–1975," *Harvard Educational Review* 49, no. 2 (May 1979): p. 146.

32. Ibid., p. 168.

33. Ibid., p. 168, note 86.

34. Quoted in Butts, *American Education in International Development*, p. 111.

35. Alan Pifer, "Response to Edward H. Berman," *Harvard Educational Review* 49, no. 2 (May 1979): 181–182.

36. John Masefield, *Poems* (New York: Macmillan, 1955), p. 195.

Date Due

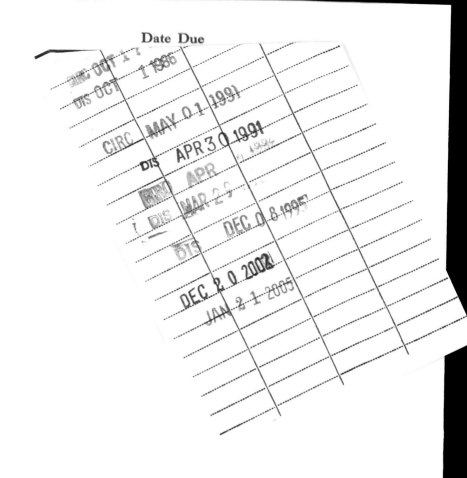